Kickstarter Handbook

STEFANO L. TRESCA

SEAHORSE PRESS

Kickstarter UK Handbook
Published by Seahorse Press
Copyright © Stefano Tresca, 2014
ISBN: 978-0-9931095-1-5

All rights reserved. No part of this book may be reproduced in any form without permission in writing from the author. Reviewers may quote brief passage in reviews.

While all attempts have been made to verify the information provided in this publication, neither the author nor the publisher assumes any responsibility for errors, omissions, or contrary interpretations of the subject matter herein.

The views expressed are those of the author alone, and should not be taken as expert instruction or commands. The reader is responsible for his other own actions.

The author may use affiliate links in the book. This means if you decide to make a purchase, the provider will pay a commission. The author doesn't keep these rewards, they are used to support young startups.

Table of Contents

10 THINGS TO DO BEFORE KICKSTARTER

13 HACKS FOR MAKING A SUCCESSFUL VIDEO

CREATING YOUR MEDIA LIST

YOU HAVE A LIST OF BLOGGERS, NOW WHAT?

MOVE YOUR MEDIA LIST TO THE NEXT LEVEL

HOW TO SET UP PLEDGES THAT SELL

8 THINGS TO DO AT THE BEGINNING OF YOUR CAMPAIGN

12 MARKETING HACKS FOR YOUR

CAMPAIGN

6 THINGS TO DO AFTER THE CAMPAIGN ENDS

KICKSTARTER UK FOR NON BRITISH

TEMPLATES

USEFUL LINKS AND RESOURCES

From my old keynotes

The Most Dangerous Phrase

The most dangerous phrase in any language is: "We've always done it this way."
– GRACE HOPPER

When I returned to London in 2010, angel investment wasn't as popular as it is today. A great team with a great idea can build a great prototype, but it's very hard to compete with the US and Asia without a proper budget. The common advice was to "take my time". Europe is different – they said – everything is slow and steady. There is only one problem: I can't accept the status quo. I never had. I don't think I ever will.

Fund raising is easy for big companies. During my years working in corporations we raised millions, even billions a couple of times. But what about small companies and startups?

That's when we started using crowdfunding: Kickstarter and Indiegogo to build products and Seedrs to raise money for equity: an entire world of backers and small investors ready to help us, or to provide quick and inexpensive feedback if we got it wrong.

4

Things have changed and raising funds for startups is becoming easier. But every few months or so, one exciting product jumps out from the accelerators where I mentor, or from the amazing startup community; and that product is perfect for crowdfunding. Then I know that it's time to start another campaign.

I don't have any magic recipe for success, but I'm happy to share what I've learnt over the years. And if during your campaign you grasp something new, drop me an email or a tweet. I would love to hear your feedback. Until then I leave you with a quote from Judith Faulkner, founder of Epic Systems.

Do good, have fun, make money.

– STEFANO L. TRESCA

* * *

The author doesn't retain any income for himself. All revenue from this book is used to support young startups.

About the Author

Stefano L. Tresca has 15 years of experience in startups of every kind, from telecom to online banking, to very traditional businesses such as steel (India), energy (Italy) and solar panels (China).

He joined his first major startup in 1996 as employee no. 8 of Wind Telecomunicazioni, later sold for €12.1 Billion. That didn't make him rich, but it gave him the opportunity to work and travel in over 50 countries over the next 10 years.

Stefano is currently based in London, where he enjoy working with startups, mentoring for a few great accelerators, reading too many books and trying to be an agent of change. Feel free to contact him on Twitter (@startupagora) or Linkedin.

Twitter: twitter.com/startupagora

Linkedin: linkedin.com/in/stefanotresca

4+1 Questions to Ask Before Joining Kickstarter

Question Zero: Kickstarter or Indiegogo?

If opportunity doesn't knock, build a door.
– MILTON BERLE

Why is Kickstarter better than any other platform? It's a common question but a wrong one. In truth, not every company should apply to Kickstarter. Sometimes other platforms are more appropriate, other times crowdfunding is not the best option at all.

Just two examples I've been involved with:

1. Metal Gear Solid the movie will be on Indiegogo.com because the team is outside the UK and they can't move out of the country (more about this project in the marketing chapters).

2. When we want to raise funds through equity–I mean selling company shares not products–we usually use Seedrs.com (disclaimer: I'm an investor in Seedrs).

As a backer, I've pledged to many projects on Kickstarter but I am on Indiegogo too. The tech and business community is probably bigger on Kickstarter but–for instance–research and nonprofit projects are forbidden. On the other hand, these projects are very hot on Indiegogo. A stem cell trial by the Tisch MS Research Center of New York was able to raise $317,540 on Indiegogo in just 30 days.

Which Chapters in This Book Can You Use for Indiegogo?

Some of the chapters are specific to Kickstarter. For instance Kickstarter is are available only to some countries. If you want to launch a campaign on Kickstarter in Europe you probably need to open a company in the UK. There is an entire chapter dedicated to this subject.

After you read this book if you decide to switch to Indiegogo you can still use the chapters about media promotion, marketing and the case studies. Moreover, some of the case studies are from Indiegogo. Winning crowdfunding requires specific skills no matter the platform you use.

There is one exception though. If you decide to use your own platform, you don't need to pay commission to anyone (apart from credit cards). However be aware that it's a completely different game.

Or You Can Build Your Own Platform

The key to success for everything in business, science and technology is never to follow the others.
— MASARU IBUKA, Co-founder of Sony

There are a few very successful campaigns that refused to use both Kickstarter and Indiegogo. The best example is Star Citizen, an online game designed by Chris Roberts, creator of the legendary Wing Commander.

Chris used his own platform raising an incredible $55 million and entering the Guinness Book of World Records. Between the Kickstarter fee and the Amazon commission—the payment service used by Kickstarter US—he saved at least $4.4 million in fees. Not bad!

There are many software providing the same features as Kickstarter, including a couple of free open source platforms. So when is the best time to use them?

My suggestion is simple: don't do it.

Unless you are mini Chris Roberts, with fame and followers, you can't raise money by yourself. Kickstarter has a massive community of loyal backers who check the website on a regular basis.

The same Chris Roberts raised an initial round of "just" $2.1 million on Kickstarter before fixing his platform and building an amazing marketing team.

If you use your own platform, I'm pretty sure you will fail. But that's what's interesting in being an entrepreneur: if you believe you can make it, it's your duty to prove me wrong. In 2013 Rob Wijinberg raised $1.7 million to start De Correspondent, a Dutch online newspaper. I still advice against using your own platform, but don't let anybody convince you that your dreams are too big.

Campaigns from This Chapter

- Start Citizen – proprietary platform
  http://robertsspaceindustries.com
- Start Citizen – Kickstarter campaign
  http://kck.st/RXG0Z8

The 4 Questions

Success is often achieved by those who don't know that failure is inevitable.
— COCO CHANEL

After the short overview of the different platforms it's time to decide if you can really benefit from Kickstarter. There are four questions that help me decide if a project is suited or not. Some are basic, and you probably know them already, some are more sophisticated.

If you have a different checklist let me know. Eventually I could add your expertise to the book quoting your name. My contact details are on my website:

http://startupagora.com/help

Question 1: Do I Have a Product to Pre-sell?

If you'r not working on your best idea right now, you're doing it wrong.
– DAVID HEIEMEIER HANSSON, creator of Ruby on Rails

No matter what they say, Kickstarter is NOT a funding platform. In typical funding a startup gives up some piece of a company (equity) to investors in exchange for money, and hopefully for some support, connections, and any other non-monetary help ("smart money").

Backers Are Not Investors

Backers don't "invest". In fact, Kickstarter doesn't allow you to give away company shares. The definition "funding platform" can be rather misleading.

Backers Are Not Donors

Backers don't donate either and charity projects are expressly forbidden by the guidelines. Even when a backer chooses the minimum pledge of $1 he has to receive something in return: a simple thank you message maybe, but there must always be something for them or your campaign risks to being suspended.

The True Nature of Kickstarter

Kickstarter is neither a place for funding your company, nor a place to pledge for donations. Its true nature is completely different: Kickstarter is a pre-sales platform, although a very unique one. This is why your first job is to determine if you have a product to pre-sell.

You don't need an "existing" product in fact in a typical campaign you pre-sell a product that doesn't exist yet. But you need to have a specific product in your mind. Customers like me are passionate enough to help you build something new. The risks are high and we have to wait months to receive the pledge. Sometimes the product is a failure and we don't get anything at all. Looking at this scenario, it's easy to understand why I need to know exactly what you want to build or I'll never commit to paying in advance.

In crowdfunding the magic word is "crowd" while

"funding" is just a consequence.

> *Kickstarter is a marketplace*
> *(a) to pre-sell products before they exist*
> *(b) to customers open to paying in advance*

What You CANNOT Do on Kickstarter

You can't launch your new law firm on Kickstarter in exchange for 3 months of consultancy for the backers. You can't offer memberships, haircuts, or personal training. You can't ask for donations. You can probably use crowdfunding for all these projects; however Kickstarter is not the right platform. You should look for a different website, such as Seedrs.com (disclaimer: I am an investor in Seedrs).

What You CAN Do on Kickstarter

In order to be accepted on Kickstarter you need to offer a product (a piece of hardware, an album, a video game etc.). And even then not all products will be approved by the Kickstarter guidelines.

If you don't have enough funds to develop your product, or to develop it quickly enough, then Kickstarter is the right place for you.

Just a Product Is Not Enough . . .

Because the core of Kickstarter is a community of customers open to paying for a product that doesn't exist, having something to offer is not enough. The product should excite the backers or they will never take the risk.

#TIP — A low price is rarely exciting unless it's so different from the market price that it's a game-changer in itself. (What if you could launch a clone of Oculus Rift for $99?)

Question 2: Do I Have the Time to Market My Project?

We are what we repeatedly do. Excellence,
then, is not an act but an habit.
– ARISTOTLE (384-322 BC)

There is nothing worse than a failed project on Kickstarter. In the same way that it can promote your startup to millions of customers, it will also advertise your failure.

Let's consider these three things:

1. You don't want to meet a potential investor and have to explain why the backers have pledged over $10 million for a paper watch but didn't want your product. (The paper watch is Pebble and we'll study its winning strategy in the next chapters.)

2. Setting up a company and getting approval from Kickstarter can be a pain — a double pain if you live outside the US/UK, although I've included a few tricks to reduce this torment in the book.

3. Marketing the campaign is the biggest pain of all. A project is usually online for just one month, but you will probably start working at least two months in advance, and will have to keep leveraging on the

campaign in the following month. You should plan (at least) on four months of hard work.

If you don't have the time to invest in a massive campaign it's better to postpone your use of Kickstarter.

How Much Time Is Required for a Campaign on Kickstarter?

In short: at least four months.

Here is a typical overview:

1. Pre-Kickstarter: Months 1 and 2 (at least part-time). Prepare the campaign, get accepted by Kickstarter, make a list of journalists and bloggers in your market etc. (More on this in the following chapters.)

2. Kickstarter: Month 3 (full-time). This is going to suck every atom of energy you have; be prepared to work seven days a week. Cheers!

3. Post-Kickstarter: Month 4 (full-time). Maximize your fame, set up a website to sell directly, understand who your typical backer is, and contact similar prospective customers etc.

You will need more time for bigger projects, of course, and you can probably invest less time if you are an influencer in your niche, or if you have found an influencer to help you. Community and influencers are two of the key tools you will need to succeed on Kickstarter.

Things are changing quickly and crowdfunding is becoming more competitive. A few years ago a nice video and a one-month campaign were enough; today some entrepreneurs suggest spending even more than four months on a single campaign, up to six months or more.

There is a saying that crowdfunding is like a marriage without a prenup and you can lose everything. If you don't know how to manage it properly ask for help before the "wedding".

> *Crowdfunding is like a marriage without a prenup. Love is in the air but you can lose everything if you are not committed.*
> *– Crowdfunding 101*

Feel Free to Drop Me a Question or Two!

I don't make a living by consulting on crowdfunding projects but I'm happy to share what I know.

When I am not traveling I am online twice a week to support early startups and crowdfunding projects. The best way to reach me can be found on my website:

http://startupagora.com/help

For me, it's a way of keeping in touch with some of the coolest people out there (you?) and to have a sneak peek at some of the best crowdfunding projects.

However if you need a full time consultant or

partner, I'm NOT your man. I'll be happy to suggest the most appropriate person for your project, if I can.

Question 3: Is My Business Too Local?

The only thing worse than starting something and failing . . . is not starting something.
– SETH GODIN

I've been asked this question by many entrepreneurs: "Is my business too local for Kickstarter?"

My answer is usually "no, never."

The general idea is that Kickstarter is a platform for international businesses, and this is true: it can give worldwide visibility for no cost.

Despite this, local businesses can be very powerful on Kickstarter. For local campaigns Kickstarter becomes a sort of escrow service: it's easier to be reported on local media. Local newspaper and radio are always starving for local news. Contact them and most of the time you'll get an interview.

With Kickstarter any local who hears about your campaign can make an impulse purchase with one click. Without Kickstarter, even if they are interested, they have to find your shop in the city (if you have one), or they have to enter their address and credit card details into an unknown ecommerce. Not surprisingly the conversion rate for local projects on Kickstarter is easily 10-20 times higher.

True Story: Meet Emilie and Her Tea Pot

It's never to late to be who you might have been.
– GEORGE ELIOT

Emilie Holmes of Good & Proper Tea raised enough money to buy a food truck and sell tea on the streets of London. No matter how many US customers saw her project it's fairly improbable that a guy from Texas would send money to fund a lady selling tea in London.

Crowdfunding is not necessarily worse for local businesses than global projects, and sometimes they can even be better. After all, you can always expand through franchising later.

Emily and her 1974 Citroen H van. (Image source: Good &
Proper Tea Kickstarter page)

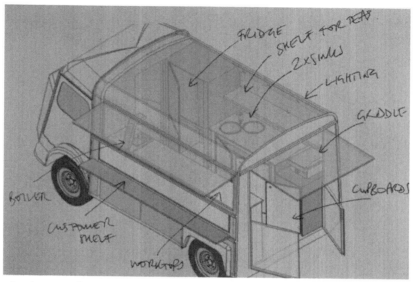

An image from the campaign. The handwritten notes add a personal touch: being the underdog always pays off. (Image source: Good & Proper Tea Kickstarter page)

Campaigns from This Chapter

- Good & Proper Tea: London-based loose-leaf brew bar (By Emilie Holmes)
  http://kck.st/WZWZQl

Question 4: Do I Need the Funds?

Whatever you're thinking, think bigger.
– TONY HSIEH, founder of Zappos

This is a common question asked by many entrepreneurs, and ... it's completely wrong. Even if you have enough funds to start a company it may be a good idea to use Kickstarter anyway, for three reasons.

1. The Very Nature of Kickstarter

You pre-sell something that you haven't built yet and your customers pay you before you pay the providers. That's a heavenly scenario for any company. Moreover, at the end of the campaign you know exactly how many customers you have, and how many products you have to make.

2. The Very Nature of Kickstarter Customers

People open to paying for something that doesn't exist are easily the best customers in the world.

That's also why "emotional" products work best. I will never buy a boring legal manual on Kickstarter but I have backed comic books and video games in the sci-fi and gothic fantasy genres—even if I don't have time to read or play them—just because I love to see them succeed.

3. The Very Nature of Kickstarter's Relationship with the Media

Kickstarter and other well-known crowdfunding platforms can promote your existence to millions of customers.

Look at Ego Smartmouse, one of the companies that I worked with. They developed their business idea in Italy with no international connections, but when they registered with Kickstarter they were featured on TechCrunch, Mashable, VentureBeat, CNet, Business Insider, ZDNet, Fast Company, and too many others to mention, including TV channels (yes, the good old traditional TV), newspapers (the kind still made of paper), and of course by bloggers both big and small from everywhere.

This level of promotion doesn't come easy. The team at Ego did an amazing job, investing an incredible number of hours every week dealing with bloggers and media agencies. And yet they didn't pay a cent in advertising. Kickstarter doesn't supply free gifts but excellent levers.

Ego Smartmouse on Techcrunch

Update: After having successfully shipped their

product to the backers, the team at Ego Smartmouse has decided to focus on other personal projects. Interesting fact: one of the reasons they switched to different personal projects is because of a job offer made by an international company to the CEO after—guess what?—their campaign on Kickstarter.

Campaigns from This Chapter

*   Ego Smart Mouse (by Laura Sapiens)
    http://kck.st/13jNyOV

10 Things to Do Before Kickstarter

The Most Important Action to Succeed on Kickstarter

Perseverance is not a long race; it is many races one after another.
– WALTER ELLIOT

What is the most important thing to do on Kickstarter? This is probably the question I get asked most by project creators. I'm not a guru–and I'm skeptical when I see self proclaimed "gurus"–but I've followed a good number of campaigns, and I have my preferred answer. Actually the answers are three:

1. Find "your" customer (just one)
2. Find "your" blogger
3. Make the right video (not necessarily an expensive one)

At the end of this book you will find an entire set of templates to help you manage customers and bloggers. But first we need to understand who we are looking for.

This chapter is a step by step guide to finding the right customer, planning a budget, and all the other things to do before starting a campaign. However I've so much material about building a media list and making a video, that they get their own dedicated chapters. It's going to be a long journey, let's roll!

1. Find One Customer

*If everyone is your customer, then no one
is your customer.*
– Old saying

"The target audience is males and females aged zero
and up"–this is a common joke among investors. When
startups pitch their businesses to us there is always one
or more company aiming to sell to "men and women aged
zero and up". They don't use these exact words but they
don't have a specific customer in mind either, or–worse–
they want to sell to "everybody".

Guess how many times I've seen these startups find
investors? You probably know the answer: ZERO.

A Wrong Target is Better than No Target

You don't want to be like those startups; you want to
have a specific target customer in mind. In our line of
business even having a wrong target is preferable to not
having a target at all. With a wrong target you can quickly
develop a dedicated offer, quickly test it, and–if it doesn't
work–quickly move to another business model or onto a

different target customer.

On the contrary when "everybody" is your target you'll get stuck in product development forever–you can't make everybody happy–and you simply don't have the resources to be marketing to everybody. It's painful I know; I made this mistake many times at the beginning of my career, and–shame on me–I've repeated the same mistake again, always with a painful outcome. Lesson learned!

Not One Type of Customer but One Real Customer

If you are planning to raise funds on Kickstarter you probably don't have a team to develop a sophisticated market analysis. The good news is: this is fine, you don't need one.

You're not Coca Cola, you don't need sophisticated data–you just need a real customer. The best tactic I've found is to sit down with paper and pencil and think about a REAL person. It doesn't have to be someone you know but you can, and you should, get inspired by real people.

Avoid an academic demographic such as "male, single, between 20 and 30, high income etc."; paint a picture of a real person in your mind instead:

"James likes to play fantasy role games with his

friends. He's a manager in a big corporation with a good income but the job is very stressful and/or frustrating. So they don't just relax with paper and dice, they go large, they use miniatures and a professional gaming table. ____ KEEP WRITING ____".

James is more or less the typical customer of Reaper Miniatures who raised $3.1 million from an initial target of just $30,000. Having funded 10,565% of their goal Reaper Miniatures is one of the most successful campaigns in the history of Kickstarter, and I strongly suggest everybody interested in making a campaign spending an hour or two checking out their video, the description and–especially–the almost 100,000 comments and interactions with the backers.

Now Multiply that One Customer for Each Pledge

This one customer is your main target and you should create a pledge around him/her. This is going to be your core offer, the one you promote to online magazines, bloggers and on social media.

The next step is to make a list of other "real" customers and match one specific pledge to each of them. We'll go back to the pledges in a dedicated chapter but here are a few examples.

Let's say you are making a movie about a Marvel

Superhero, you will have a number of fans NOT interested in your movie–they preferred the official production, or maybe your character is not their favourite–but they still want you to succeed. A $1-5 pledge is best suited to them.

When it comes to superheroes you always have (more than) a few people passionate about cosplay and memorabilia. They'll be ready to pay quite a premium for the costumes worn during filming. A $200-500 pledge is most appropriate for them, and if you have a strong community or a famous actor involved, the pledge could easily be much more than that.

2. Browse Your Email and Facebook

Vision without execution is hallucination.
– THOMAS EDISON

In a typical campaign 50% of your backers come via word of mouth through friends and family. In the age of the Internet and online marketing we forget that word of mouth is still one of the most powerful weapons in our arsenal. Best of all: it's free.

Family and Close Friends

Use and "abuse" your family, they can take it. Above all don't take them for granted; despite the family ties, many will not help unless you push them. You will be surprised by the lack of support from many, and the unexpected support of a few. The first campaign is a continual surprise and–for many of us–a life changer. You'll see a charming cousin best-friend-forever who won't even pay $1 yet a grumpy uncle sending $1,000 (true story).

This is what we usually do:

1. Browse your email and Facebook and make a list 2 weeks before the campaign starts. Last minute lists are always incomplete and stressful. Besides, the week before the launch may be so tense that you won't want another unfinished task hanging over you.

2. Prepare a draft email, one email for each person. Never ever send an email to multiple people. More in the template chapter at the end of the book.
    Exception: a single email might work if you contact an entire family, such as "your uncle, his wife and kids". Save the draft for later use.

3. A free resource like Streak (www.streak.com) allows you to save any number of draft emails directly in your Gmail inbox and automatically send them on the day of the campaign. They also have templates.

4. Don't use the same title for every email or they will be blocked as spam. The number of your family and friends is limited so you should be able to create different subjects in the title line (hint: using the name of the receiver in the subject is an old trick but still works).
    For emails with the same subject line you can schedule different sending times with Streak.

This paragraph is all about a core number of family and close friends, a circle small enough to allow you to draft a dedicated message. For "other friends" and acquaintances use a mailing list service such as Aweber (http://bit.ly/listaweber).

You can find more in the template chapter at the end of the book.

How to Identify Your Worst Enemy

That's simple. In a crowdfunding campaign your worst enemy is YOU. In a typical campaign, word of mouth generates an average 50% of the revenue but many entrepreneurs are ready to give up half of their income to avoid embarrassing situations with their family or best friends. They are embarrassed to pitch their product to people they know.

I understand that family is more important than business and you don't want to ruin your relationships. On the other hand they are your family and best friends. If you don't have the courage to propose your idea to them, how can you convince strangers?

When it's time to ask for help from your family and close friends there is only one rule: don't be a stalker. Besides that, be shameless and persistent. You will be surprised how far you can push yourself when you get into the right frame of mind.

Other Friends and Acquaintances

The very moment that your campaign becomes visible to the public you are supposed to flood your network of friends, acquaintances and coworkers with emails. If you can generate a great number of social media shares and pledges in the first four hours you can only win. Best case scenario, you get featured on Kickstarter's home page, generating a viral effect and impressing bloggers. Worst case scenario, you will still impress many bloggers, and they will cover your story.

In order to succeed, every email should be ready to send in advance. The second that your campaign is visible to the public you won't have time to write anything, you just need to click a button or two. Luckily, you don't need an expensive army of virtual assistances. You can reach this goal with a set of templates and a couple of free apps.

This is what we usually do.

In the weeks before the start of the campaign we make a list of email addresses for all the acquaintances and coworkers of every member of the team. It's a simple 3 column Excel spreadsheet:

1. Name of the member of the team
2. Name of the contact
3. Email of the contact

Possibly we populate the list by asking for more names from our sisters, brothers, fiancées, wives, husbands, best friends, everybody including our mums. Don't be shy, they are your family and friends; they can take it.

Minimum list: 1,000.

If you have less than 1,000 contacts keep digging. Get names from your cousins, best men, bridesmaids; anyone you can think of. We all agree that you don't have to ruin a relationship for your campaign. Besides that (almost) anything goes. Being shameless is a plus.

This number–1,000–is not mandatory; you can choose to pick a smaller goal or a bigger one. It works for me because it's big enough to require a decent effort and good teamwork, but at the same time it's not so big to be unreachable. You don't want the team to fail their first task and lose their enthusiasm.

If you are managing the campaign by yourself–this is very common among writers fund raising for their book– or it's just two of you with not many connections, you can reduce the goal to 500 contacts or less. If in doubt I would prefer to be bold and set a high goal. You will be surprised by how much you can achieve when you set a challenging goal.

How to increase the conversion rate by up to 500%

When you have reached a good number of contacts

go to a mailing service like Aweber (http://bit.ly/aweberUrl) or Mailchimp (http://bit.ly/mailchimpUrl) and set up one different list for every member of the team. This way when you start your campaign every contact will receive a message from an email address they know and trust. Moreover, if they have saved the sender's email address, there is less risk of it being blocked by their spam filter.

As an alternative you can create a single long list and send an email signed by the entire team. There is no mandatory rule, it's your call. However, I've noticed that when we send emails from multiple lists and every contact receives a message from an email address he knows the conversion rate is 3-5 times higher than a generic email.

3. Estimate the Cost

Don't ask for what you want. Ask for what you need.
— Crowdfunding 101

Kickstarter is a "win-all/lose-all" platform. If you reach 99.99% of your goal you don't get anything. ZERO. On the other hand you could raise more than 100% of your goal. Think back to Reaper Miniatures who raised 10,565% of their initial goal, more than 100 times what they needed.

Despite the long list of Kickstarter successes there is one piece of information rarely made public. Many entrepreneurs lose money on Kickstarter, even when their campaign is successful, or—should I say—because their campaign is successful. Unexpected international shipping costs and inconsistent quotes from manufacturers are the main two reasons for this.

Here is a list of costs to consider and some tips for reducing your risk.

- **Manufacturer cost** (of course). If you haven't used the manufacturer before don't assume that their time and cost estimation is anywhere near the truth. Befriend and ask other entrepreneurs producing a similar product instead. Websites like

Alibaba could be particularly helpful.

- If you have a digital product you don't have traditional manufacture problems or a shipping issue. But unless you develop everything by yourself you will still have to deal with programmers and such. Try to involve an experienced project manager, or–if you don't have the budget–befriend and chat with a couple of them. Buy them dinner or a drink; this will be one of the best investments of your campaign (and eventually you may make a new friend).

- **Shipping cost**. Hint: don't consider the weight of your product alone. Consider the wrapping and the box, plus any other gadgets you promised to include.

- **Duties**. Don't forget that many countries will charge duty on imports. Digital products don't usually have this issue and it's the same for books and comics (but beware of shipping a comic which contains nudity to some countries; the consequence can be much worse than a duty tax). The websites and local branches of UPS, DHL or other providers can be very helpful. It's a complex matter, so it's better to check different sources.

- **Storage**. A warehouse could be more expensive than you think.

- **Kickstarter commission and other fees**. When your project reaches its goal Kickstarter takes a 5% fee for each successful charge. If you go through Amazon Payments you will get charged another 3%-5%.

- If the charge is unsuccessful because the backer has an issue with his credit card or simply decides to cancel his support, you don't get anything from them. Between the Kickstarter commission, Amazon and/or credit card fees, and unsuccessful charges, you should consider a total cost of 15%-20%.

#TIP – As a rule of thumb, calculate all necessary costs and add 20%. That's your initial goal.

#CALL TO ACTION – Do you have any other experiences not included in the list? Contact me and I'll update your suggestions in the book, citing your name (if you like). The best way is through Twitter or my website http://startupagora.com/help

Don't Ask for More But Aim for More

If you don't reach your goal even by one cent you don't get anything. Thus aim low and ask for exactly what you need to cover your costs. You can always raise more than your goal.

In fact a limited goal could help you to raise more. It's easier to reach 40% of a small sum and this percentage is usually the trigger that pushes more backers to support your project–nobody wants to side with losers. Once these backers help you reach 100% of your (limited) target it's easier to convince bloggers and online magazines to write about you - and that drives even more backers to your project.

Exception to the Rule

Kickstarter is not just a fund raising platform but also a great marketing tool. If you plan on developing your product anyway it could be convenient to set a goal smaller than you need.

If you "just" reach your goal you'll have to put your own money into the product, but you would have invested your money anyway. Kickstarter provides a down payment and an incredible marketing window. And if you raise more than your goal, you can eventually cover all the costs.

The opposite is also true although unusual. In some rare cases the project creator sets an impossible goal to reach in order to create buzz and free promotion. They are not ready to create the product so they use Kickstarter to "test the water" and create some buzz for the future.

I'm not recommending this strategy; I just believe that it has been used before. Ubuntu Edge–a campaign I supported on Indiegogo–raised more than $12 million and still failed. They set an impressive goal of \$32 million. I don't know if they planned on a high chance of failure from the beginning, but they got impressive coverage throughout traditional and social media.

4. Prepare Your FAQ

I hated every minute of training, but I said "Don't quit. Suffer now and live the rest of your life as a champion".
– MUHAMMAD ALI

Once the campaign goes public you will spend a large part of your time replying to comments on the Kickstarter page, on social media and in the comment areas of the blogs that covered your story.

This can be very time consuming. You can save a lot of time having a short list of FAQs or at least the answers to the main questions. You can add them to your Kickstarter page and use them to reply to the comments. Ask your friends and coworkers what's not clear about your project - you will be surprised by some of their reactions.

The FAQ can be changed and improved during the campaign, based on interaction with the backers and blogs.

#TIP – When a blogger posts about you thank him in the comments and switch on the email alert to follow the comment stream. This allows you to keep an eye on feedback and potential new customers, not to mention shady competitors aiming to damage your reputation (there are way too many of them).

5. Do (Not) Build a Community

Creativity is thinking new things.
Innovation is doing new things.
– Startup 101

Many stress the importance of building a community to be successful on Kickstarter but they forget one element. There is simply not enough time during a campaign to build a (traditional) community.

You either have a community or not. Amanda Palmer and her band–a true story covered in the book–had an impressive community before their campaign on Kickstarter. But the largest number of creators start with a small number of followers on Twitter and a group of Facebook friends–this is especially true for smaller projects.

#TIP – You don't want to postpone your project until you have a solid community. Building a community takes a long, long, long time and you can't afford to lose momentum.

Leverage Kickstarter to Create a

Community

If you don't have a community before you start your campaign you can leverage Kickstarter to create one. You don't have to wait until the very last day. You start your campaign at least two months in advance so use these months to create a group of followers.

If you are launching a comic, you can publish your draft on Tumblr, together with drafts from other authors with a similar style (but check the copyright first). You can replicate the content on your new Facebook page (Facebook has more users, but I would not suggest focusing your entire campaign on Facebook for as you know, it's impossible to reach all your followers on Facebook.

If you are launching a webcam to control your cat when you are not home (true story) you could start a Pinterest profile all about cats. And so on.

There are exceptions–of course–and you have to decide if you are one of them. However, building a solid community could easily take one year and I strongly doubt that any entrepreneur can afford to lose all that time.

True Story: Meet Maya of Rain - A Fan Film about Storm

*Kickstarter is not just a funding platform,
it's a marketing platform.*
– Crowdfunding 101

Check out Maya Glick at RAIN: A fanfilm about Storm. She is not a famous actress with hundreds of thousands of followers. On the contrary, she's a mother who lost her son and decided to create something unique: a movie about her favourite hero.

How many people knew about her story before Kickstarter? I guess not many. By the time the project was funded she still had less than 1,000 friends on Facebook but her "tribe"–to use Seth Godin's word–had grown enough to fund a small $10,000 project . . . twice.

Like many other first time entrepreneurs she was hit by extra costs during the shooting of the movie–first of all insurance. Maya went back to her tribe for a second shot, many members of the tribe contacted their friends– this is how I got involved by the way–and the movie is back on track. Thanks Kickstarter!

Campaigns from This Chapter

- RAIN: a fan film about Storm (by Maya Glick)
  http://kck.st/1sLbw3a

6. Rearrange Your Website Specifically for Kickstarter

Home pages are becoming less relevant.
Stories have to stand on their own.
– HAMISH McKENZIE columnist of
Pandodaily

Do You Need a Website During the Campaign?

There is an ongoing discussion among Kickstarter veterans about the creator's website. I'm not talking about your Kickstarter page but about your personal or company website.

1. Some say that during the campaign you should forward the URL of your website to your Kickstarter page. Thus whoever types your website address into his browser is directed to your Kickstarter. The timeframe of a campaign is limited and every extra pledge counts.

2. Others say that your website should be separate. Your Kickstarter page lists your website and some

backers will click this link to find out more about you. They don't want to be forwarded back to where they came from.

Personally I tend to prefer the second option. But it's really your call.

A simple forward is fast and it doesn't require any maintenance during your campaign, a time-frame where you need all the time you can get. On the other hand, when the campaign ends you are still an entrepreneur and you still have to sell your product. If you have used your website as a simple forwarding URL all the traffic collected during the campaign is lost. Visitors will not be used to going to your website and you have to start everything over from scratch.

Do You Need a Website Before the Campaign?

Whatever your decision during the campaign I strongly suggest having a website at least until the campaign starts. The time-frame between the moment that you decide to go on Kickstarter, and the moment that you effectively activate the campaign could be a very long one. You need to plan the costs, analyse the market, prepare a media list, and much more. During this time, you don't have a Kickstarter page yet and you can benefit greatly from a website, or at least a landing page to collect the email addresses of potential backers.

If you are into writing, you can add a blog although this tool is less effective in crowdfunding than in other businesses considering the limited timeframe of a Kickstarter campaign.

No matter how many pages your website has if you plan to go on Kickstarter the home page should be very simple. Your goal is not to impress and generate traffic; you are not selling ads here. The first goal is to collect emails with a dedicated field such the one provided by Aweber (http://bit.ly/listaweber). The secondary goal is to convert them into followers on social media. Or maybe you want to invert these two priorities if you are particularly good with social media. In any case the goal is to try to establish a connection with as many potential backers as possible. People who are simply curious are fine too because they may spread the news among their friends.

On the first day of the campaign you'll contact them all. It's critical that you raise money and create buzz during the first days of the campaign. If you do so you'll get press coverage and maybe your campaign will be featured on Kickstarter's home page.

In short, you don't need a website for the sake of it but to use as a tool completely focused on creating buzz and getting pledges during the campaign's first days.

When the campaign ends you can transform this website into your ecommerce platform. A link to your website at the top of your Kickstarter page will bring extra free traffic for a long time.

How to Get More Backers' Email

You don't know if your page is really performing until you A/B test it. That means creating two or more alternative home pages and comparing their performance.

If you already have experience in web marketing this is nothing new to you. If you don't you probably feel overwhelmed. You have to develop a video, a media list, and who knows how many other things, and you don't think you have the time to develop two or three alternative home pages. I understand how you feel.

On the other hand I've seen A/B testing improve the performance of a home page by up to 600%. If you don't have the time or the skills to do it quickly by yourself, you can get it customised for a few dollars.

The service I'm using at the moment is Optimizely (http://bit.ly/optimizel) but I'm sure there are others out there.

You can create alternative pages in a few minutes and without any skills. The most complete version of Optimizely can be expensive but you don't need it. Besides, a campaign is just one month long plus the timeframe before the launch. You can always cancel the monthly fee as soon as the campaign ends.

7. Set Up Your Company

We have to design companies for the way we are, not the way we wish we were.
– ROELOF BOTHA, Sequoia Capital

If you don't have a company now's the right time to set one up. Unless you are an author promoting his own book, or a similar exception, never start a crowdfunding campaign without a company. If you are an entrepreneur you probably have a company already. In which case you should decide if it's more convenient to use your existing company or set up a dedicated one. Here is a list of thoughts in no particular order:

1. First of all you need a company to reduce your liability. If you fail to deliver the product or–worse–the product hurts someone, they will sue the company, not you. There are some exceptions but if you haven't lied on purpose or acted with extreme negligence, you are usually safe. I'm not going to go into detail because this is not a law book and because this is not specific to crowdfunding. If you have any doubts contact a lawyer. Lawyers might not have a soul but they do have bills to pay and sometimes a family to feed. (By the way don't tell these types of jokes in front

of me. We lawyers can be very touchy!!!).

2.   You need a company to look professional. If you really believe in your project you plan to stay in business long after the campaign ends. If you don't have a company you are sending a very bad message to your backers. If you don't believe that your business is here to stay for the long term why should they?

3.   As usual there are exceptions. An author that wants to fund raise for his new book might not need a company. These exceptions are fewer than you think, for instance the author of a comic book should probably set up a company since customers who buy comics are used to having a relationship with a brand not a person. (They adore Stan Lee but they buy from Marvel).

4.   If you are an entrepreneur and you have a company already have a think about setting up a new dedicated company for Kickstarter. This is not the best choice for everybody. The choice usually depends on the comparison between the existing product and the campaign. For instance a company producing videos could use Kickstarter to raise funds for another video or set up a new company. Both are fine. However a web marketing agency producing an app should probably open a new company because the two businesses are quite different.

5. If you already have a company to decide whether you should open a new company consider the long term. For instance, if you are an app developer and you plan to launch a game changer such as Angry Birds in gaming or Hootsuite (http://bit.ly/socialmana) in social media, it's probably better to start a new company. With a dedicated company it's easier to raise money from investors, split the shares with dedicated co-founders and employ a dedicated team. Kickstarter can be a great place for startups to test their products before they look for equity investors. Think about Oculus Rift, they launched their virtual reality headset on Kickstarter and they were acquired approximately one year later by Facebook for $2 billion. They didn't just present themselves as a group of brilliant engineers; instead they acted as a company from day one and got rewarded for that. An impressive $2 billion reward.

If you plan to set up a company in the UK see the last chapter for more technical advice.

8. 9. 10. You Are Almost There

Most people overestimate what they can do in one year and underestimate what they can do in ten years.
– BILL GATES

Kickstarter is a long journey but–don't worry–you are almost there. There are a few additional things to do before you start your campaign:

8. Make the right video

9. Find the right bloggers

10. Create the right pledges

I've so much material and so many true stories about these actions that they all deserve a dedicated chapter. The next five chapters are all about them.

Creating a media list with the right bloggers and making a video is incredibly time consuming. So I am not being completely honest when I say that you are almost there. The aim of the following chapters is to make your life easier.

13 Hacks for Making a Successful Video

Video Used to Be Our Most Important Marketing Weapon. What Has Changed?

If you do not change direction, you may end up where you are heading.
– LAO TZU

You have heard that video is the first factor in the success or failure of a Kickstarter. This is not completely true anymore. A few years ago the number of projects was limited, and backers like me were used to checking every video every week. Thus a good video meant life or death for a campaign.

Today, Kickstarter is packed with projects, and backers rarely see yours unless they have heard about it in the press, on social media, or – even better – on the home page of Kickstarter as one of the featured projects.

In the Marketing Chapter we are going to cover a list of hacks to be featured on the home page. Developing a media list, contacting bloggers before the campaign starts, and using tools like Thunderclap helps to bring good traffic and many pledges in the very first days.

Good results give you a better chance of being chosen as a featured project by the staff at Kickstarter, which means a huge spike in traffic and pledges. It's not as easy as it sounds, but it's possible. Even if you don't get featured, that's the way to go.

After all this planning and promotion, however, video still plays a major role in converting visitors into backers. What has changed is that you can't use one video alone.

1. Video should be part of a media and social media strategy.

2. Your main video should be connected to a series of secondary mini videos. Don't worry, they will be easier to make than you think. We'll check out a few hacks together in the next pages.

I could write an entire book about the theory behind promotional videos, but I prefer to show what works through real case studies.

1. Be Personal, I'll tell you how

People follow people, not ideas.
– Old saying

There is a famous quote: "People follow people, not ideas" and its modern version: "People follow people, not companies". They are both very true on Kickstarter. Indeed, the entire platform is based on trust, not on products.

Backers send money to someone who they don't know, for a product that doesn't exist yet. So your first goal is simple to identify but hard to execute:

Before selling your product you have to sell yourself.

This goal is difficult for any business. In crowdfunding it's even more difficult because you don't have a product at all. In a Kickstarter video it means 3 things:

1. Show your face;
2. Tell your story;
3. Explain why you want to create the product (Hint: "I want to be rich" is not the right answer).

Amanda Palmer raised $1.2 million with a video almost entirely shot by her alone in front of the camera -

and she is not even talking!

Amanda Palmer raised approximately $1.2 million, an impressive 1,192% of her goal. (Image source: Amanda Palmer's Kickstarter page)

Pebble raised $10.2 million with an initial goal of just $100,000 with a similar approach. There is more video time spent showing the team than the product.

Pebble Kickstarter Video

Show your face. (Image source: Pebble Kickstarter video)

DREAM TEAM

Pebble Kickstarter Video

Show your team and tell your story. (Image source: Pebble Kickstarter video)

No matter how shy you are you can't succeed on Kickstarter without covering these three points in the video.

1. **Show your face** and the face of your team. We'll see in the next pages how to manage the team in the video.

2. **Tell your story**. Casey Hopkins raised $1.2 million for an iPhone dock, with an initial goal of just $75,000, focusing the entire video on his personal story in his dad's machine shop.

3. **Explain why YOU want the product**, not why you want to sell the product. There is no product yet, remember? Maybe you are not satisfied with the market standard and you want to develop the product for yourself like Casey Hopkins. Or maybe you want to cheer on your heroes like Andrew Pascal, who shot a documentary about the creator of Dungeons & Dragons, and was sued by the company that owns the rights to the game.

Whatever your reason, it should be personal and exciting. Crowdfunding is not about business, it's about passion.

Funded! This project was successfully funded on February 11, 2012.

12,521
backers

$1,464,706
pledged of $75,000 goal

0
seconds to go

Project by
**Casey Hopkins +
ElevationLab**
Portland, OR

2 created · 47 backed

Has not connected Facebook

elevationlab.com

Casey Hopkins raised $1.46 million with an original target of just $75,000, an amazing 1,593% of his goal. (Image source: Elevation Dock Kickstarter page)

KICKSTARTER   Discover   Start   Search projects

The Great Kingdom is the subject of an intellectual property dispute and is currently unavailable.

No need to check the servers — the rest of Kickstarter is doing just fine.

Have a question? You can ask the project creator.

Thanks for your patience.

Andrew Pascal and his friends got sued shooting a documentary on the origin of Dungeons & Dragons. (Image source: The Great Kingdom Kickstarter page)

Campaigns from This Chapter

- Amanda Palmer: The new RECORD, ART BOOK, and TOUR (By Amanda Palmer)
  http://kck.st/JliwH9
- Elevation Dock: The Best Dock For iPhone (By Casey Hopkins)
  http://kck.st/uu4Ty8
- Pebble: E-Paper Watch for iPhone and Android (by Eric Migicovsky and Pebble Technology)
  http://kck.st/HumIV5
- The Great Kingdom, the Creation of Dungeons & Dragons (by Andrew Pascal and Others)
  https://www.kickstarter.com/projects/720223857/the-great-kingdom

2. Pick the "Face" of the Project

Success is the ability to go from one failure to another with no loss of enthusiasm.
– SIR WINSTON CHURCHILL

I often get questions about the team. "How many minutes should I spend on my team in the main video?" or "Do I have to make a dedicated video to present my team?"

When we pitch a startup to investors in traditional funding we spend up to one third of our time talking about the team, sometimes more. This is not how Kickstarter works, and backers are not traditional investors. They don't invest in a company, they buy a product.

So the answer is "Yes, you still need to introduce the team but not spend too much time talking about them" and "No, you don't need a specific video about the team". In fact you can do much better than that. You should focus the main video on one person and the product, and split the team up, featuring them in further low cost videos.

One Project, One Product, One Face

When you shoot the main video for a campaign it works much better if you pick one person to represent the entire team. He/she will be the "face" of the project. This is a well known tactic among companies (think Richard Branson of Virgin), and also TV newscasts and political parties.

If you have a company the Face will be probably the CEO, however this is not mandatory. If you are not British you might want to pick the person who speaks the best English.

I've even seen CEOs dubbed on a couple of occasions. It's easier than you think and it doesn't blow your budget if you use an online service. We tend to use Voice Bunny (http://bit.ly/voicebun) but I'm sure you can find others if you don't feel they are the right fir for you.

Kickstarter allows you to upload only one main video which it features at the top of the campaign page. This will be the most watched and the most embedded by bloggers and online magazines.

However, there is no limit on how many videos you can embed in the page description. This is where multiple mini videos about the team make your project more human and increase the level of trust for your product. Just upload these videos to YouTube or Vimeo, and embed them in the page with the same technique you would use for a blog.

True Story: Meet Alessio and Loka the world of fantasy chess

If you have more than three priorities, then you don't have any.
– JIM COLLINS, Good to Great

"My name is Alessio Cavatore. I worked as a game designer for almost 20 years designing miniature war games such as Warhammer, the Lord of the Rings, Kings of War and many others".

This simple quote is at core of Loka, a fantasy chess game. The video is lean and low cost. Alessio talks for just 3 minutes in front of the camera about him and the game. That's it.

And yet the project raised around 416% of their goal. A total of $104,172 in four weeks. Picking the "face" of the campaign is one of the most important pillars for the success of your video.

Campaigns from This Chapter

- Loka: the world of fantasy chess (by Alessio Cavatore and Mantic Games) http://kck.st/X2Paci

3. Split the Team Between Mini Videos

A leader is best when people barely know he exists, when his work is done, his aim fulfilled, they will say: we did it ourselves.
— LAO TZU

#TIP – Shoot mini videos with a member of your team or one of your advisors, upload them to YouTube or Vimeo, and embed in your description on Kickstarter.

You don't need to add all videos on day one. On the contrary, you probably want to introduce part of your team during the campaign. These constant updates will, by the way, bring people back to the campaign page. Even if they are already backers they will get a chance to share your campaign on their social media, or talk to their friends and colleagues about your project.

Not every visitor will watch every video, and this is fine. Over the last few years backers are getting used to spending more time surfing among projects. Having multiple videos could push them back to the page and become your backers, if they are not already.

#TIP – Mini videos are not just for your team. If during the campaign you find a new advisor or a prestigious testimonial, put them in front of the camera, and ask them why they have decided to support you. It doesn't need to be fancy or expensive. On the contrary, a genuine 60 second testimonial in front of a webcam could provide the best results.

4. Tell Your Story (Hint: Underdogs Sell)

It's not the size of the dog in the fight; it's the size of the fight in the dog.
- MARK TWAIN

Backers can order a high end product directly from Apple or Amazon's websites. They don't want to back perfect companies; they want to cheer for the underdog.

There may be a few exceptions but they usually involve a celebrity or two, such as Veronica Mars, a movie that raised $5.7 million, or Reading Rainbow with LeVar Burton, a.k.a. Geordi in Star Trek: The Next Generation. Introducing yourself as a major company doesn't work unless you have a major organization or a star in your video.

And even when a star is involved, being the underdog always pays off. Look at LeVar's Reading Rainbow page. He has the skills and the connections to shoot a sophisticated video, with special effects worthy of a Star Trek episode.

Instead the cover looks like a video that (almost) anybody could have made. The shooting is genuine and funny, and I love it. Check the bottom left corner of his video, and you'll see an impressive 872,534 shares on Facebook that endorse this strategy.

LeVar Burton had the resources to shoot a refined video. He chose a simple style instead. Being the underdog always pays off, in this case by $5.4 million. (Image source: Reading Rainbow Kickstarter page)

Pebble used the same approach. They didn't hide the background of their tech company. On the contrary, they leverage trust through transparency, such as putting their cranky prototype under the spotlight.

#TIP – Showing a prototype in your video has a double positive effect. You leverage trust through transparency, and at the same time you show that your product is not just an idea but a reality. You are "almost there" and you will respect your shipping deadline. You need just a little help from the community of backers.

Pebble Kickstarter Video

Team Pebble showing a messy prototype. It's a common tactic today, but was a bold move at the time. (Image source: Pebble Kickstarter video)

Campaigns from This Chapter

1. Amanda Palmer: The new RECORD, ART BOOK, and TOUR (By Amanda Palmer)
   http://kck.st/JliwH9
2. Bring Reading Rainbow Back for Every Child, Everywhere! (By LeVar Burton)
   http://kck.st/1kKwSrD
3. Pebble: E-Paper Watch for iPhone and Android (by Eric Migicovsky and Pebble Technology)
   http://kck.st/HumIV5

True Story: Sarah Northway and the Zombies of Rebuild

Weird stories sell.
– Crowdfunding 101

When I say that you should tell your story, I mean a real story. Explain who you are, how you got the idea, what difficulties you have overcome (and what difficulties you did not), and why you are so passionate about your project.

Some project creators take this idea quite far and create a story that is funny and weird. This is not easy, because the story should highlight your product, and you still want to look natural and professional.

It's not for every project, but if you have an unusual product, you should probably think about it. Let's check a real case study.

Sarah Northway developed Rebuild, a zombie strategy game (yes, you read that right). I don't spend much time playing on my iPad but I bought this game because the theme is unusual and I love strategy games - 42 hours non-stop on Sid Mayer's Civilization was part of my teenage years. The game sold well and Sarah decided to launch a new version with a more advanced design and animation, this time with the help of a team.

Sarah presents the game and the team, like in every other Kickstarter video. But the entire theme is based on a "Zombie-proof jungle on a remote island in the tropics where they have solar power and plenty of water, but no people – which means no zombies" (her words, not mine).

As you can imagine, with such a great story it's not difficult to convince a journalist or an existing customer to have a look at your video. Which means also having a look at your page, where the pledge button is just a few centimeters away.

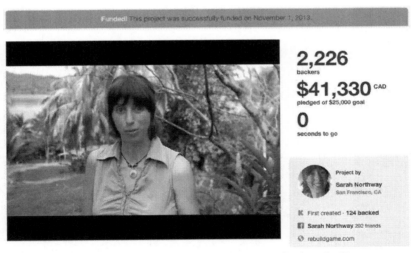

Sarah Northway and her zombie proof island. (Image source: Rebuild Kickstarter page)

Rebuild is not the only campaign using this tactic. There are many impressive videos made to resemble newscasts or funny stories but I've picked Sarah for a simple reason.

Her video was almost free to make. Like many digital nomads Sarah lives and works part of the year outside her native Canada, and the video is a simple mix of her in front of the camera and screenshots of the game.

You don't need an impressive budget for Kickstarter, if you don't have one. Just a camera and some creativity. Do you want another example? Have a look at Double Fine Adventure, they raised over $3.3 million and their video has no animation or special effects.

Campaigns from This Chapter

- Double Fine Adventure (by Double Fine and 2 Player Productions)
  http://kck.st/A9k3jH
- Rebuild: Gangs of Deadsville (by Sarah Northway)
  http://kck.st/1bomFhU

5. Don't Explain the Features of Your Product

"Here's what our product can do" and "Here's what you can do with our product" sound similar, but they are completely different.
– JASON FRIED, Founder of Basecamp

This is counterintuitive, but true. Don't explain the features of your product, SHOW THEM!

With Pebble you can play music on your iPhone and get notifications of messages and emails while playing sports. It sounds almost normal now but these were highly innovative features in 2012, the year of the campaign. Their video doesn't explain how the product works; it shows real people using it.

There is more. None of the customers in the video look like a supermodel or an Olympic champion. They are all "normal" people, just like your backers.

#TIP – If you want to put someone else besides you in the video, avoid actors who look like a top model. Backers want to see themselves using the product. The cliché of the girl next door is a bit cheesy, but it works every time.

Pebble Kickstarter Video

Show as many real life users as possible. (Image source: Pebble Kickstarter video)

6. Anticipate Their Questions

If you are not embarrassed by the first version of your product, you've launched too late.
– REID HOFFMAN, Founder of Linkedin

A cool watch is suddenly not so cool if the battery runs out every couple of hours. Pebble dedicated an entire scene to address this concern. And they didn't stop there. They show that the screen works well in sunlight. They show a prototype to prove that the product was "almost there". The entire Pebble video is used to anticipate questions.

The team at Pebble didn't invent the questions; they asked their friends and colleagues instead. Then they integrated the answers into the video. Conducting a survey is time consuming, but with $10.2 million raised in 30 days I'm sure Team Pebble don't regret the extra time spent.

Do you have to hide negative

answers?

It's easy to promote a 7 day battery life but what about negative features? A typical sales guy would suggest hiding every bad element of your product; personally, I don't think that's a good idea.

My suggestion isn't based on moral grounds – although that's an important aspect for many of us– but on a pure business analysis. Kickstarter is a pre-sales platform which means that raising the target of your campaign is not the end of your journey, but the beginning. You should grow your business and keep selling quite a while after your campaign has ended.

The media exposure attached to Kickstarter could work against you, if you have cheated the backers. Moreover, if there is a smart, innovative lawyer out there I bet that class actions for fraudulent crowdfunding campaigns are right around the corner. (Book aside, if you think you are that innovative lawyer, contact me. Maybe we can do business together.)

It doesn't mean that you have to be naive. Between lying and being stupid there is always a third way. If Pebble's battery had of lasted just a few hours they would have probably come up with a slogan such as "Don't worry about the life span of the battery. It's 4 hours now but with your help we'll manufacture a 7 day battery– shipped free to all our backers!"

Anticipate their questions. (Image source: Pebble Kickstarter video)

7. Add a Call to Action

If I had asked my customers what they wanted, they would have said a faster horse.
– HENRY FORD

All the successful campaigns have something in common: the project creator expressly asks for help. Phrases such as "Help us to reach the target" and "Click the pledge button on the right of the video" are very common among winners.

It may be obvious to you that you are asking for money, but backers are surfing the Kickstarter website and jumping from one project to another. The fact that we–backers–want to back an appealing project doesn't mean that it will be YOUR project. A "call to action" interrupts our surfing and increases the chance of transforming visitors into backers.

Asking expressly for help sounds silly but it works. Helping is the entire point of crowdfunding after all. Check out Shadow who raised 164% of their target. This is another video entirely made by one person; it's not expensive, but very effective and full of calls to action.

Hunter Lee pitching Shadow - Community of Dreamers.
(Image source: Shadow Kickstarter page)

Campaigns from This Chapter

- SHADOW | Community of Dreamers (By Hunter Lee Soik)
  http://kck.st/16asGpx

8. Add Gamification Anytime You Can

Imagination is more important than knowledge.
– ALBERT EINSTEIN

Gamification in Kickstarter usually means involving the backers in the making of the product. It's not mandatory but is always very effective

Check these two examples out:

1. **Pebble.** The makers of Pebble didn't sell the watch in 4 different colors. They chose 3 colors instead and let the backers decide number 4.

2. **Shadow.** The makers of Shadow didn't choose to launch the app on iPhone. They let the backers choose between iPhone, Android and even the less popular Windows Phone.

By the way, picking the operating system in Shadow is one of the best executed hacks I've seen on Kickstarter. The community of backers raising the most money – Apple, Android or Windows– get the app first. The others have paid the same price, but they have to wait one month or more.

In the end the iPhone community won the race at

Shadow, but for 30 days, iPhone fans and Android supporters and Windows users battled it out against each other. The only way to get the app immediately available for your phone was to convince all your friends using the same system to back the campaign too.

A side note: I wonder if the result would have been any different in the UK. Shadow is a New York based campaign, and the penetration of Android is much stronger in Europe than in the USA.

3. You don't have to develop a sophisticated pledge to benefit from gamification. Do you remember Emily of God & Proper Tea from the previous chapter? She didn't have an app or hardware to develop. But every backer was allowed to propose a name for her van. This kind of small but inexpensive idea can involve the backers in the project, and also generate buzz on social media. Win-win-win!

VOTE ON 4th COLOR

Pebble Kickstarter Video

Pebble "Vote the Color" competition. (Image source: Pebble
Kickstarter video)

Emily launched a "Name the Van" competition. (Image
source: Good & Proper Tea)

9. Add Secondary Videos

People often say that motivation doesn't last. Well, neither does bathing. That's why we recommend it daily.
– ZIG ZIGLAR

In the battle of the videos, the more the merrier.

Kickstarter allows only one main video at the beginning of the page. However you can add as many videos as you want in the description. You don't need to produce many expensive videos for the campaign, one professional video is fine, and sometimes that's enough to cripple your budget.

However, secondary videos are very effective for interviews and updates. Let's look at these two types in detail.

1. Interviews and testimonials. If you have a team, let them talk. It doesn't need to be an expensive video. On the contrary, a short genuine interview works like a charm. If you get a new advisor on board do the same. Not all the backers will look at all the videos and that's fine. The videos are there and they can lure potential backers back to your page.

2. Updates. Backers rarely read your updates, but they will often watch your videos. I would go further and send at least an update per week. Update the backers when you hit a target, show them the team at work, and inform them about your coverage in the media. Backers are paying for a product that doesn't exist yet, they don't just want a pledge; they want to be part of building something new.

3. Involving your advisers. A collateral effect of the secondary videos is to involve your advisers more in the project. They can be your best evangelists. Have a look at the Kickstarter page of SHADOW, they have used this tactic in a very effective way. Many advisers have been invited to record their point of view and upload the video.

Mike Del Ponte–founder of Soma–got used to sending regular updates to the backers. His videos are simple, fast to shoot and cost nothing. At the time this photo was taken Soma had raised 50% of the target in just 36 hours. That's a great news to share.

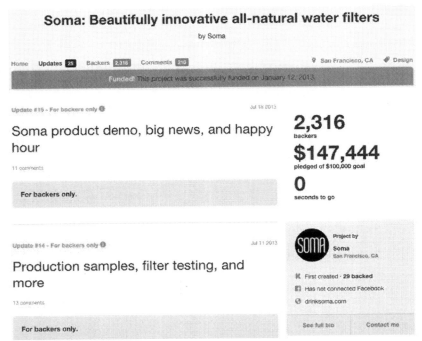

The video updates are hidden to non-backers. This reinforces the sense of community among the backers, and it creates curiosity among everybody else. (Image source: Soma Kickstarter Page)

Campaigns from This Chapter

- SHADOW | Community of Dreamers (By Hunter Lee Soik)
  http://kck.st/16asGpx
- Soma - Beautifully innovative all-natural water filters (by Mike Del Ponte and Soma)
  http://kck.st/VjAFva

10. Show Your Social Media

In the Networked Age, you're not just 'you' anymore. You're also who you know, how they know you, what they know about you, who they know, and so on.
— REID HOFFMAN, Founder of Linkedin

This is a simple hack, but one often forgotten in the main video. Social media is a very powerful tool to promote your campaign so point every person watching your video there. That's it!

It doesn't have to be fancy and expensive. Look what the team at Veronica Mars did: simple, inexpensive and effective.

Veronica Mars the movie raised over $5.7 million. Yet they added their social media to the video in a simple and inexpensive way. (Image Source: Veronica Mars Kickstarter page)

More on the Veronica Mars campaign in the next chapter.

True Story - Meet Veronica Mars

When the going gets tough, the tough get going.
– JOHN BELUSHI, Animal House

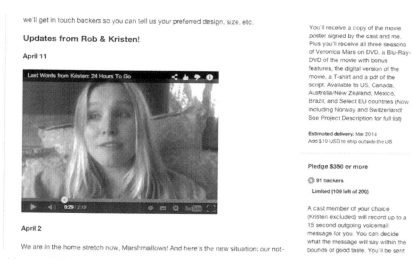

Using Kickstarter like a blog. (Image source: Veronica Mars Kickstarter page)

The image above is from the Veronica Mars Kickstarter campaign. Kristen Bell announces that they have just hit the $5 million mark. Time to celebrate and enjoy the success, right?

Wrong!

Indeed, Kristen thanks the supporters ... for less than half of the video. Then she delivers the news that–yes they have broken the record for the highest amount of funding ever raised–but not the record for the highest number of backers. In other words, there are projects out there with less money but more supporters. Hey, that's terrible!

So Kristen invites every backer to convince one friend to make a $1 pledge. Even if they don't have the budget or are not interested in the movie, they can still make a difference. After all $1 is a small price to pay for your friendship.

In case you are curious, after this message the campaign raised an extra $702,000. Not all the funds came from the $1 pledges, but they surely played their part. Not a bad result for a few minutes in front of your webcam, don't you think?

3 Hacks with 1 Click

There is one obvious lesson to learn from Kristen's video.

1. Ask for the help of your backers, it's simple as that.
But there is more.

2. Don't just ask for help, provide detailed instructions.

3. Use a small pledge to get email addresses.

These points both deserve their own chapter, and this is exactly what I'm going to do in the next pages.

Campaigns from This Chapter

- The Veronica Mars Movie Project (by Rob Thomas)
  http://kck.st/Z1HJRR

11. Don't Just Ask for Help, Give Them a Wish List

I hear and I forget; I see and I remember; I do and I understand.
– Chinese Proverb

Veronica Mars didn't ask for generic help. The request was extremely specific: "Ask your friend to pledge $1".

Fans tend to react best when they have clear instructions. Sure, there will always be someone more creative developing their own tactics. You don't send your message to these supporters; in fact they will find a way to help you in any case. You send a specific suggestion to anybody else, including someone who is usually creative but simply too tired or too busy.

The easier you make the life of your backers, the more they'll expend time and energy to support you.

In our example suggesting a pledge of $1 is brilliant. The sum is small enough to not scare anybody and you don't risk losing the higher pledges; on the contrary, once the friends of your backers are on your page they can decide to spend more.

12. Use a Small Pledge to Get their Emails

Anyone who has never made a mistake has never tried anything new.
– ALBERT EINSTEIN

For the sake of privacy you don't have access to the email addresses of your backers, but you can still use Kickstarter to send direct messages to them. Team Veronica Mars gained access to hundreds of thousands of email addresses with their $1 message.

Even if the sum is small you can reach all your backers, and you have until the end of the campaign to convince them to upgrade their pledge. I'm not talking spamming here. Sending exciting updates works like a charm.

In the meantime they can share your updates with their friends and social media. It's an army of evangelists; one of the most effective marketing engines and one of the most rewarding experiences from a personal point of view. Don't ignore them, don't spam them, instead cuddle them and feed them with amazing updates, videos and funny emails.

13. Which Video Sells the Most?

Humor comes from self-confidence.
- RITA MAE BROWN

I'm often asked what themes sell the most in a video. Short answer: humor.

There is a famous quote from Rita Mae Brown "Humor comes from self-confidence". The contrary is also true. The less confident you are the more you try to compensate and end up looking stilted and overly professional. The sad consequence is a long line of videos with the speaker looking like a bad imitation of Mark Zuckerberg.

Kickstarter is not pitching to the venture capitalists in Silicon Valley. Besides, humor can help in front of the investor as well. I've seen it many times. Check out Drew Houston, the founder of Dropbox, you can find his application to the startup accelerator YCombinator on the internet (Google "Drew Houston Dropbox application YCombinator"). The tone is funny and informal and you can read a couple of jokes too.

Go back to LeVar Burton's video where he enters schools by surprise and enjoys the reactions of the teachers. It's staged but who cares. It's funny!

Ok the shock looks staged, still the video is funny. (Image source: Reading Rainbow Kickstarter page)

Which Video Sells Second Best?

Perhaps humor won't work for your project, although I doubt it. In this case there will be no 'second best' theme. You have to find the theme most appropriate for your project.

However no matter the theme you choose never ever look overly professional. There is a slogan we often repeat in consultancy. It's "Crowd + funding" not "Crowd funding YOU". You are either part of the crowd or outside the crowd. In the latter case it's very unlikely that anybody will care about your project.

What's Happening behind the Scenes

As a startup CEO, I slept like a baby. I woke up every two hours and cried.
– BEN HOROWITZ, serial entrepreneur and venture capitalist

For the sake of privacy the general public can't access your video analytics. It's the right choice—and I applaud this decision—but sadly it means that you can't access the analytics of your competitors either.

It would be very useful to study similar projects before making your own video. Luckily Kickstarter made the video analytics for some successful campaigns public, and I've seen quite a few projects too. There are two pieces of insider news that are the outcome of these campaigns.

1. First outcome: few people watch the entire video. Have a look at the analytics for Pebble and Amanda Palmer. Only half of the potential backers watched their videos until the end, and these are both majorly successful campaigns, with excellent videos. In less successful campaigns the percentage is even smaller.

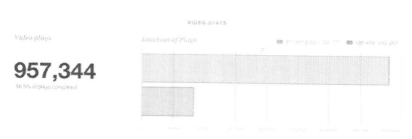

Video Analytics for Pebble. Source: Kickstarter.

Video Analytics for Amanda Palmer. Source: Kickstarter.

You can see the immediate consequences: you need to have a great beginning to your video and get straight to the point.

This is the opposite of a traditional keynote. A traditional business school would suggest spending the entire first part of your keynote detailing a market problem. Only after that, do you introduce your solution. That probably worked in the past when managers had the chance of getting a long meeting with their board of directors. It doesn't work on Kickstarter, where the attention span of the typical backer is around 12 seconds.

And it's not just Kickstarter. It's very common that startups have to pitch their entire business in 30 seconds, and it's a fact that recruiting agencies spend an average of less than 20 seconds on every resume. Everything moves fast, and we are caught in a kind of "adapt or die" scenario. It's not just crowdfunding; using a quote from Brad Feld of Techstars —one of the top startup accelerators in the world entrepreneurs have to "do more faster"

2. Second outcome: most potential backers will watch your video directly on your Kickstarter page.

If you are doing well in public relations the video will be embedded by bloggers and online magazines as well, but this will only be a fraction of the views.

The reality is that one of the most successful tools on Kickstarter is to be featured by Kickstarter itself. This is a result usually achieved by directing high traffic and backers to your page during the first few days. We'll talk more about this in the marketing chapter.

Video Checklist

There is no finish line. So love the journey.
– DAVID WEEKLY, Founder Pbworks

Here is a check list of must-do's that we use to develop the campaign video. If you have anything to add, contact me. I always appreciate a good tip. My contacts are online: http://startupagora.com/help

Kickstarter Video Checklist

❏ Who's the "face of the campaign"?

❏ Who is behind the campaign?

> *Speak about you, your motivation and introduce your team. Explain why you the right person to bring this project to life.*

❏ What will be the end product? What unique benefit will it provide?

❏ Who is your typical backer? Why should they be interested?

❏ When will the backers receive their pledge?

> *This information should be very clear.*

❏ How are you going to spend the money?

❏ What will happen if you exceed your goal?

Many creators promise extra features or faster development if the campaign reaches a higher goal. More about stretch goals in the Pledge chapter.

❏ Final check: Does the video get to the point?

There is nothing worse than a creator blathering for the entire video.

Other Elements You Might Want to Define

❏ Will you accept backers outside your country?

This is especially useful for physical products.

#TIP – You can edit the video after the campaign has started based on the feedback and questions from the backers. For instance when Laura Sapiens launched their campaign for an intelligent mouse we didn't completely agree on the storyboard. The beginning of the video was very technical, including a description of the operative system. Not exactly what excites the typical backer. After the initial feedback this part was cut and a new amazing video uploaded (with my somewhat guilty pleasure).

Creating Your
Media List

Start Small, Sell Big

You don't need A media list but YOUR media list.
– Crowdfunding 101

Every startup I know wants to be featured by TechCrunch – and that's their first mistake. They are geeks, they read online magazines for geeks, and they want to be celebrated by their own community of geeks. I admit I can be quite geeky too; my profile on Kickstarter is full of pledges for hardware–not always useful–and for movies about Star Trek and Star Wars. However the goal is not to get page views or important covers, it's to make sales.

Sure, the home page of Wired helps your sales, but that's not the goal, it's just a tool. I know, I've been there. Every campaign I've followed has been featured by some of the main geek magazines, including TechCrunch, Wired and AOL, and most of the time the main sales didn't come from them but from a couple of unexpected blogs, from Reddit or from an interview in the local media.

One of the startups I follow–Laura Sapiens–developed a futuristic mouse for geeks and gamers, so being featured on TechCrunch was the right call. But they were the exception not the rule. Before you start emailing any major websites out there, the first step is to develop a tailored list of bloggers–for three reasons:

1. The obvious reason: It's easier to get featured by a smaller blogger than by a leading website.

2. Second reason: Unless you have very good connections in the media the best way to be featured by a leading website is to be highlighted by many smaller bloggers. Almost every writer at the Huffington Post, Wired and TechCrunch looks for new ideas by surfing the Internet. If you want to see great examples in action, read "Trust me, I'm Lying" by Ryan Holidays, the best book ever about this bottom-to-top marketing strategy.

3. Third and most underestimated reason: a post in a blog may sell more. The readers of the major magazines are exactly that–readers. The readers of a niche blog are much more than that; they are "followers"–in the good sense of the word–and part of a community. They will be more open to buying/downloading/supporting anything that is introduced by their community leader–the blogger.

Now we've agree that we need to look for bloggers the first part of the problem is solved. There is a second problem though. There are a few major magazines, and millions of bloggers. If you are planning to use Kickstarter, you're not a big corporation and you don't have the resources to contact many of them.

Good news, you don't need to. The step by step process in this chapter and the templates should make your life easier.

Templates and More

In this chapter I refer to many tools and templates used in many campaigns. They are all attached at the end of the book. You can also find the Word and spreadsheet versions on the website:

http://startupagora.com/crowdfunding-templates

Feel free to download them and to change them. But don't make them overcomplicated. They have been tested and simplified many times before becoming what they are today.

Why You Don't Need a Blog

Look for the blogger, not for the blog.
– Crowdfunding 101

I want to go one step further in this bottom-to-top marketing strategy. It's not just about starting from (relatively) small blogs and moving up to the top online magazines later; the right strategy is about looking for specific bloggers.

At the beginning of the blog revolution there were a few top writers with their own personal blogs. Bloggers were rare and readers were hungry for new posts—usually to be enjoyed at work. These days are long gone, and writers tend to publish on multiple platforms: their personal blog, various online magazines, social media or shared platforms such as Medium.com.

So when I use the word "blogger" I mean both people writing in their own name, and journalists writing for leading online magazines. In the current market they are often the same. Professional journalists are becoming a rare breed, while most writers publish on multiple platforms.

Sometimes they are bloggers without a blog. Mike Elgan is a great example; he has abandoned his personal blog in favor of micro-blogging on Google Plus—not the most 'trendy' social media platform, I know, but a paradise for geeks and photographers. Mike has over 3.5 million followers on Google Plus, he has his video podcast and writes for many magazines, from Computerworld to Datamation and everything in between.

In short, what we should look to introduce our Kickstarter campaign to is a "blogger" not a "blog". If Mike Elgan writes many posts about wearable and smart watches (he does), and you have a product in this area, you should contact him, not the magazine which he writes for. If Mike is interested in your product he'll find a place to publish his article, you don't need to. (Plus, he'll share his article with his 3.5 million followers on Google Plus).

3 Tools for Creating Your Media List

If I had nine hours to chop down a tree, I'd spend the first six sharpening my axe.
— *ABRAHAM LINCOLN*

The sub-engines of Google and Kickstarter itself will help you to define a list of bloggers with a higher potential for your campaign.

1. Google Blogs Search

Find bloggers that already talk about your kind of product. Find the best keywords to describe your product, market or idea and use Google Blogs Search:

http://www.google.com/blogsearch

This is one of Google's least known sub-searches. You'll get a great list of blogs. The best results are those labeled 'blog homepage for [keyword]'.

Google Blog Search

#UPDATE – The portal "Blog Search" above was discontinued in May 2014. However the blog search engine still works. You can access the engine by typing the application for the Blog Search into your browser's address bar manually:

http://www.google.com/search?tbm=blg

There is no guarantee that Google will not discontinue this service in the future. If so, I'll disagree but respect their decision. In the meantime, happy hunting!

2. Google Images Search

Another useful sub-search engine is Google Images Search:

http://www.google.com/imghp

If you click the image of the camera in Google Images

Search, as in the image, and upload a photo from your computer you'll find any page on the internet that shows the same photo.

Google Images Search

In order to use Google Images Search for Kickstarter you just need to find an existing campaign similar to yours. I usually start with a list of between 5 and 10 campaigns that are currently running or are from the not-too-distant past.

Download their photos and conduct a search on Google Images. You'll find every web page on the internet showing the same photos – and generally that means a full list of articles written by bloggers and journalists about them. I've never seen a post about a campaign on Kickstarter without one or more photos of the product taken from the project's Kickstarter page.

Once you have the names of these bloggers it will be easier to engage with them. Because they've shown interest in a similar product in the past, there is a good chance that they will be interested in yours.

Reading their post about the similar product, gives you a great opening line when you contact them. "Hey Joe, I read and enjoyed your post about [old project on

Kickstarter] on your blog".

Personally, I tend to be honest and don't flatter the blogger as it will sound unnatural in later conversations. But you can use any approach you like. Just be natural.

3. Kickstarter Hidden Stats

Once the campaign is online you can use the Kickstarter hidden stats to find out who's talking about similar products.

To find the hidden stats for every campaign, click the embed button under the video. Copy this short link into your browser adding a + at the end. For example if the short link is "http://kck.st/JliwH9" copy "http://kck.st/JliwH9+". The reason why this works is explained in more detail in the next chapter "7 Things to Do at the Beginning of Your Campaign".

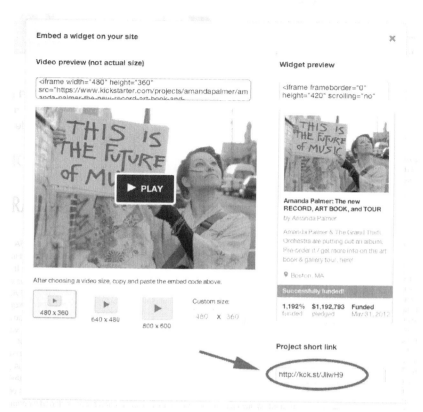

Copy the short link and add a "+" at the end. You'll find out who's taking about the campaign, including bloggers.

We are not concerned about your campaign stats yet. In this phase, your campaign hasn't started and we are building a media list of bloggers and journalists to contact later. In fact we are talking about similar campaigns' stats.

Make a list of features and keywords for your future campaign (It's an app or a game app? A fantasy movie or documentary? Etc.), then check past and existing campaigns with the same features and keywords.

Their hidden stats are a goldmine. You can find what social media will probably work best for your campaign, which blogger writes about similar products, and much more.

For the goal of this chapter—building a media list—the hidden stats could take you to the original article and thus provide 3 powerful pieces of data:

1. The name and contact details of the bloggers
2. The name of the publication (a personal blog or an online magazine)
3. The URL, title and date of the article (you'll use this referral when emailing the blogger to prove that you really read and enjoyed his/her article).

But don't start taking notes about all this data just yet. Just register the short links. In the next pages we'll see how to outsource this time consuming research for just a few dollars.

It's Not Just About the Product

Searching for similar campaigns to build a media list is not just about searching for similar products. In fact, it's more about searching for similar interests.

So if you plan to launch a fantasy game app for smartphones you should not look just for campaigns for apps in general (same product) but about gaming and fantasy (same interest). If a blogger writes about fantasy movies and books, he will probably write about your fantasy app as well. People are moved by passion and expertise, not by business areas.

#TIP – Looking for campaigns by product is very useful during the ideas stage, even before you develop a media list. For instance, one of the startups I deal with developed a fantasy universe through a collective of writers and then some fantasy battle rules. What they hadn't decided yet was whether to utilise these stories and rules and make them into a card game or an app. With just a few hours of research we saw that card games tend to perform very badly on Kickstarter—with some exceptions—and the idea of the card game was abandoned (well, at least for now).

True Story: How to Promote Your Campaign through Bloggers. Meet Doug and Jimmy of Minaal

> *In preparing for battle, I have always found that plans are useless, but planning is indispensable.*
> *– DWIGHT D. EISENHOWER*

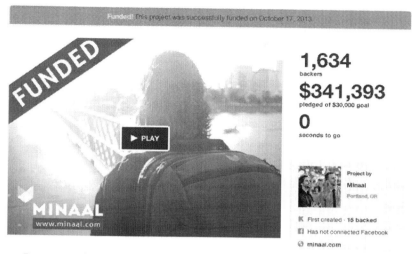

Doug and Jimmy of Minaal raised 1,100% of their goal.
(Image source: Minaal Kickstarter page)

One of my favorite campaigns among my pledges is Minaal, a travel bag launched by two friends from New Zealand. Doug and Jimmy raised 1,100% of their goal in 30 days. This is not a typo. They raised 11 times the amount of money they were looking for, with a media strategy mainly focused on specific bloggers.

Besides being one of their backers I have no business connection with the campaign. Well, maybe there is one connection. Like me, Doug is a lawyer who decided to stay away from big law firms and start an unusual journey.

These two friends spent a few years travelling the world—a passion which can drain your savings account, unless you refuel your wallet from time to time. Being a lawyer, Doug planned to consult a few times per year but he found it hard to charge a respectable fee when meeting his potential clients whilst wearing a backpack! Lawyers are supposed to be serious and boring–at least that what they used to tell me all the time!

To cut a long story short they were looking for a comfortable travel bag that would also look like a smart business case. They couldn't find one, so they decided to make it. That's when they joined Kickstarter.

With a target of $30,000, Minaal raised an impressive $341,393, more than 11 times the initial goal. We're not talking about a famous marketing guru or a movie star here, but a lawyer, albeit a funny one (yes funny lawyers exist … although they can be a rare species sometimes) and a campaign with a very limited budget.

How to Raise 1,100% of Your Goal

Having a great product is not really helpful if nobody knows about it. Doug and Jimmy didn't have a marketing budget, or hundreds of thousands of loyal social media followers.

What they realized is that they didn't need an impressive budget to purchase Google ads, nor did they need to create a group of loyal followers. In fact they just had to pitch their idea to a limited number of people in their niche market: let's say 100 travel bloggers. They–the travel bloggers–already have thousands of loyal followers each.

I can't credit Minaal's success to their media list alone. They had an excellent idea for a product, the capabilities to create it, and great interaction with their backers (I still receive funny newsletters from them). However I believe their media list is the root of their success.

A few niche bloggers reach a smaller number of readers than a top website but the percentage of conversion—readers who become backers—is impressive. You don't need page views, you need sales. It's not the same thing.

Campaigns from This Chapter

• Minaal Carry-on: travel faster, happier & more productive (By Doug Barber and Jimmy Hayes) http://kck.st/14YVmaZ

You Have a List of Bloggers, Now What?

Outsource Your Research to Save Time and Money

Never mistake motion for action.
– ERNEST HEMINGWAY

Now that you have a better idea of what kind of bloggers you are looking for, you can outsource the research to a virtual assistant. Actually this is not completely correct; the appropriate phrase is "You SHOULD outsource the research to a virtual assistant". Creating a media list is extremely time consuming, and if you try to do it yourself you'll delay the launch of the campaign and raise less money. Saving a few dollars by not hiring a virtual assistant is going to be a very expensive mistake. You probably think that you can be the exception–that's what I thought at the beginning–but I've seen many projects in the last few years and the results have been always the same: outsourcing these kinds of jobs is way better.

Personally I use oDesk.com–a website specializing in contractors–but there are many platforms out there. Just pick the one you like.

By the way . . .

If you are already familiar with the concept of virtual assistants, feel free to skip to the next paragraph.

If not, I already know what you are thinking. You are planning to use Kickstarter because you don't have enough money, so why do you have to spend what little budget you have to outsource something you can do by yourself?

Well, I like to answer this with a real conversation I had with a startup (the first sentence is taken word by word from his email).

Mike: "I can do the research myself and use the $5 per hour saved on the contractor to buy Google Ads".

Ok, let me understand. You are a programmer making at least $60 per hour. So you have two options. First option, you spend the entire day doing data entry, and save $5 x 8 hours = $40 for a virtual assistant. Second option, you sell your services to an agency, you earn $60 x 8 hours = $480, pay the virtual assistant and still have $440 to spend on Google Ads.

If you don't outsource these kinds of repetitive jobs, you are not saving money, you are losing it. If you are concerned about unemployment in your country, or simply by the different time zone, don't be. Many contractors from your country are online as well, and they are often worth the extra cost.

If you have never done a crowd funding campaign

believe me. It will suck out every atom of energy you have. You can't waste time on data entry, nor on anything else that you can outsource and automate.

We Love Templates

At the end of the book, you can find a set of templates to manage your virtual assistants. I am sure there are other templates out there, but I've tested these ones myself. Feel free to suggest any improvements; you can find my contact details here:

http://startupagora.com/help

The latest version of the documents is online on my website:

http://startupagora.com/crowdfunding-template

If you want to go the extra mile about how to use a virtual assistant, I strongly suggest two e-books:

- **"Start Small, Stay Small" by Rob Walling**. This is a must read for every startup, even if you don't want to stay small but grow later.
- **"Four Hour Work Week" by Tim Ferris**. Even if you don't agree with the author's vision of the world, the chapter on virtual assistants is simply brilliant.

What You Can Outsource and What You Can't

The first rule of any technology used in a business is that automation applied to an efficient operation will magnify the efficiency. The second is that automation applied to an inefficient operation will magnify the inefficiency.
– BILL GATES

Web Research and Data Entry

One activity SHOULD be outsourced all the time: web research and data entry. I'll repeat it again: never ever do web research and data entry by yourself. It doesn't mean that you will never make any research, in fact I suggest spending many days surfing similar projects and reading articles to decide what you want to launch on Kickstarter and see if there is a chance of success.

However, once you have decided you will outsource web research and data entry–including the creation of a media list according to this chapter and the templates.

If you don't have the budget, consider interrupting your project for a few days to find the money. A virtual assistant costs a few dollars per day; it's going to be much more expensive to delay the project because you want to do everything by yourself.

Copywriters, Developers and Other Professionals

Depending on your project, you may need the help of a specialized professional, such as a copywriter or an app developer, etc. These are specialized skills and fall outside the traditional concept of virtual assistants.

Personally I don't like to completely outsource specialized skills; I prefer to spend some time and setup a core team. For instance, I'll agree to employ a developer on oDesk.com only if we have an in-house CTO or a developer. He will control and coordinate the contractors.

There are always a few exceptions to the rule and I've seen some projects succeeding despite the complete outsourcing of some core skills. It's not a path that I like to suggest and I think that they were successful just because the owner was extremely good at coordinating the external contractors.

In short, you can decide to delegate core skills if you

want. There is no official rule, it's your call. However, I've rarely seen these campaigns succeeding.

Sales and Promotion

You can't completely outsource sales and promotion. Period. The PR agencies will disagree, but I strongly believe this. Sales and promotion are part of the life of an entrepreneur—some would say that they are "the" life of an entrepreneur. And you don't stop being an entrepreneur at the end of your Kickstarter campaign; on the contrary, the end of the campaign is sometimes the beginning of your life as an entrepreneur. It's better to learn to know when you have a specific platform and higher interest from the media.

Having said that, I'm not against employing a PR expert to support your campaign. They will work with you, not just for you, and eventually you'll learn from them. If your project is hardware or tech there are quite a few ex journalists willing to work for an acceptable deposit and a payment upon success. Just think of them as a strategic partner, not simply a consultant.

Employing a PR expert is mainly a matter of balance. You don't need one to raise $5,000 to write your novel. For this amount, it's better to do the job yourself.

My personal suggestion: go out and talk to potential customers yourself. Getting doors slammed in your face can be better than a degree. Actually I've done them both. I've a J.D. and a Master, but I can swear that I've learned more going outside the office to look for funding and customers. The goal is to get the door slammed in your face so many times that you stop fearing failure. That's when you start feeling better, much better.

What You Should Never Outsource

In theory, anything can be outsourced. You can be tempted to delegate any contact with the media to focus on your "real job". This is especially true for developers and engineers, who feel that sales are a pain, or worse, something for a less talented person.

Truth is: you can't outsource being an entrepreneur.

Taking decisions–not necessarily connected to the product–and selling is the main job of an entrepreneur, and you can't completely outsource that. Especially not on Kickstarter.

Even if you want to focus on being a developer or an engineer, my suggestion is still the same: go out and sell. The reaction of your potential customers or investors is invaluable feedback on your product.

Outsourcing for Non English Speakers

Hire good people and leave them alone.
– WILLIAM McKNIGHT, Chairman of 3M

Many of my friends and customers don't speak good English (and I'm being kind here). The reason is in my background. I was born in Italy, left the first time when I was 18, and since then I've worked and/or travelled in 54 countries. Now that I'm back in London I always have some non-English friends or acquaintances who want to move here. Sometimes they want to relocate (London is an exciting city), sometimes they just want to start a business (it's tough to raise funds in Southern Europe).

Some customers can't speak a great of English either, but they can usually understand it. And with so much English media out there you can't manage a successful campaign on Kickstarter without using the English language.

The issue is that if you join Kickstarter you are now an entrepreneur and can't completely outsource sales and promotion. You can't lose touch with the customers. What to do then? It's a tough question and I don't have an easy answer, only (good and bad) experiences. I tend to not be involved in the campaign's daily activities–

unless the company is mine—so we have tested different solutions for when the owner doesn't speak good English.

The PR Expert

We have worked successfully with former journalists now working in public relations. If your project is good, and your team is credible some of those experts may be open to working for an acceptable deposit and a success fee.

How to Draft an Agreement with a PR Expert

You don't need a 20 page contract but before the job starts you want to have at least half a page of bullet points with the following questions:

1. What will they want from you?
- Are they going to be paid monthly?
- Are they going to get a bonus if the campaign succeeds?
- Is it always going to be the same bonus? (For instance 5%) Or is it going to change based on results? (For instance 5% of the goal if the campaign succeeds and 10% on everything above the goal)

2. What are they going to provide—in detail?

- Are they going to write the emails themselves?
- Are they going to meet you once a week? Etc.

This is just some advice based on past experience. Many professionals may have a standard agreement, and some of them are becoming specialized in crowdfunding.

No matter what they propose, I like to fix part of their fee to a success bonus. You don't have to do that, it's just my suggestion.

The Copywriter

We have successfully employed a copywriter on oDesk.com to correct the entrepreneur's communications. Even if you have appointed a PR expert, there is a lot of daily communication that the entrepreneur has to do by himself. You don't want to have misspelled words or grammar mistakes.

The cheapest solution is to employ a copywriter on a need-by-need basis (by the hour). However, for Kickstarter it could be much better to employ a contractor part time and "reserve" 10-20 hours of his time every week.

My friend Grant from ScissorBoy TV—host of a TV series for hairstylist and expert in outsourcing—jokes that "Every part time contractor has 2 full time jobs". Contractors by the hour accept as many jobs as they can, plus a few more. You don't want to send an urgent message to your copywriter and find her busy for the entire week. Being fast is important in every business, even more so in a 30 day campaign. If you don't reach the goal, you don't get anything.

A fixed income could guarantee some peace of mind to the contractor, and get you a fast reply. Make it clear to the contractor that you will pay him even if there is no work to do that week (there will always be work to do anyway) but in exchange you need replies within 24 hours.

You'll find a set of templates to control and coordinate contractors at the end of the book. They have been extremely helpful to me for many years.

Move Your Media List to the Next Level

The Spray and Pray Tactic

As you climb the ladder of success, check occasionally to make sure it is leaning against the right wall.
– Anonymous

The most commonly used tactic to promote any project is "spray and pray". Make a huge list of bloggers and put their contacts into Aweber or Mailchimp. Send the same generic email to each and every one of them (the "spray") and pray that someone replies.

This may be a very good tactic for spammers, but I've never seen it bring in positive results in a crowdfunding campaign.

Worse. It is counter-productive. Many bloggers who read about your campaign later will refuse to write about you because you have been labeled as a spammer.

In short: don't do it. Period.

The Buddy Call Tactic

You miss 100% of the shots you don't take.
— WAYNE GRETZKY

The Buddy Call Tactic: a funny name for a scary concept. You are supposed to contact strangers and turn them into friends. The goal is to "Turn bloggers into buddies"; you have probably read this quote already. It's the best tactic and yet the least used by startups.

Usually startups do the opposite. The very moment they think of "marketing" they start writing traditional press releases, using an overly professional tone, looking cold and boring. Most of the time their press releases are not even read by the bloggers. Why does this happen? I guess because we are taught since childhood to be unnaturally polite to strangers. I am no exception. It took me two years working in international negotiations to lose this habit.

Plus the phrase "turn bloggers into buddies" sounds quite manipulative. And it's true, it "sounds" manipulative until you realize that bloggers and journalists make their livings sharing interesting news. Give them some real news—not a self promotional press release—and they'll be happy to write about your product.

It's not simple, and you need to learn some

storytelling. Until then, just focus on sending out an interesting story. Read your email out loud. The very moment you sound like a TV commercial, you are dead. Go back and change that story.

Back to the specifics of a crowdfunding campaign, here is a list of ideas coming from past projects.

Tips for Managing the First Contact

You never get a second change to make a first impression.
– HARLAN HOGAN

Some of these ideas may be obvious but I always find it easier to follow a complete list.

1. Read at least a few articles written by the blogger (again, by "blogger" I mean any person you want to cover your story. It could be a journalist for a big online magazine, but he/she will probably write on multiple platforms).

2. Show the blogger that you really read his article. This works especially well if the blogger has written about a similar crowdfunding campaign.

3. I often use a double message: email + tweet. You might not be a big Twitter user but—as you know—journalists tend to use it a lot.

4. Don't underestimate Google Plus. Not because Google Plus is popular—in fact it's still weaker than Facebook or Twitter—but exactly for the opposite reason. Because Google Plus is often mocked, its users have developed an impressive amount of

pride. If a journalist is active on Google Plus, he will love you for being there as well.

Dealing with Bloggers after the Story is Confirmed

Don't worry about failure, you only have to be right once.
– DREW HOUSTON, Founder of Dropbox

1. Once the story is confirmed you still have quite a lot of work to do. First of all, try to find out when the story will be published. You want to be there to tweet and share. The other readers will be more interested in a story that shows signs of success.

2. Don't just ask for the date of publication, try to influence it. A few lines in an email or a quick Skype call works best "We are launching Monday 7:30 am UK time, could you publish the story around the same time?"

3. If the blogger can't or won't publish the story the first day of the campaign, you should still try to influence the timing of publication. Remember the chapter about the best time to start a campaign: you don't want to start a campaign on the weekend nor during the holidays. The same rules are valid for publishing a story about your project: not on the weekend, not during the holidays.

4. Don't take anything for granted. If the blogger has a Facebook page with thousands of followers, ask him to post the news on Facebook too. If he has a popular Twitter account, ask him to tweet. It sounds obvious, but it's not.

5. On the other hand you don't want to become a stalker and harass the blogger with multiple requests. Finding a balance is always the most difficult thing. Personally I tend to be quick and direct. Not many people read an email when it's more than 3-5 lines long. This is going to change with some bloggers when you establish a long term relationship.

#TIP – In general the best moment to publish a story about Kickstarter is early in the morning during the first 2-3 days of the week. Millions of employees get to work and—instead of starting their job—they go online. It's cynical but true (and if you have ever worked in a big company you know it too).

#TIP – Remember the old expression "Three times a charm". Don't give up just because a blogger doesn't reply to you. The first time I sent an article to Tech City News I didn't get a reply from Alex—the editor—even though I know him personally. I went back and read my post again, looking for grammar mistakes or boring lines. Then I wrote to him again, and the post was published. I found out later that he was just busy (or maybe he was testing my commitment, I can't be sure).

Don't be a stalker yet be prepared to be quite persistent. Nowadays if I like the blogger or the magazine I send at least three messages using different media. Twitter is less ignored than an email, so my second message is usually a tweet.

If I really like a specific blogger I try to contact him/her more than three times. It's a fine balance between being persistent and being a stalker, and I admit sometimes I come very close to crossing that line.

Dealing with Bloggers after Launch

Fear is the disease. Hustle is the antidote.
– TRAVIS KALANICK, Co-founder of Huber

Launching a campaign on Kickstarter is like fighting with Gerard Butler in the movie "300": constant action without any rest. And this time, YOU are King Leonidas, even if you don't have his skills or charisma. If you think starting a campaign on Kickstarter is a hobby or a part time job, think again.

I don't have many suggestions; I only know that I have to do something practical every day or I lose my grip. Personally I tend to deal with bloggers and marketing first thing in the morning before I'm overwhelmed by emails, phone calls and meetings.

In the evenings–and sometimes in the afternoons– we go to every conceivable event connected to our projects, from a small meet up to a big conference. We always tend to close some deals–no matter how small– DURING the event. What I mean is that we try to force an action from every potential backer.

"You like it? Great why don't you pledge now? . . .

Not sure it's worth it? No problem, why you don't pledge $1 (you can upgrade it later). I really want you on board. . . . You can't because you don't have the Kickstarter app on your smartphone? No problem, why don't you submit your email on our website. You can do it now. I'll send you an update and some cool [drawings/stories/something]"

I know it looks creepy. If you have great results with online marketing, you probably don't have to meet so many people in person. On the other hand, after the campaign ends, you'll have to deal with customers and providers. Even if you are raising a few thousand Euros to fund a book, you need to promote the book after Kickstarter, dealing with interviews and meeting the readers. Your campaign is a great training ground.

When your Kickstarter campaign is running people tend to forgive almost all weird behaviour. It's better to be a bit creepy now and after 30 days of constant interaction you'll became a better entrepreneur. Eventually you'll learn how to sell with style and be charming without looking weird. I can't promise that though. After 15 years in business sometimes I'm still too pushy, but at least I don't feel ashamed any more.

How to Know if Anybody Read Your Email

When you're doing something you're passionate about, stress becomes a features not a bug.
– AARON LEVIE, Founder of Box.com

This is a hack that I suggest to every startup, not just a crowdfunding project. Whatever your business, you are supposed to regularly contact bloggers, potential customers and partners.

If you shoot out 5 emails a day (this is not a random number but a tip I learned from a great entrepreneur) you will quickly amass a pile of emails without a reply. You don't have the time to keep writing to all of them, besides you don't want to look like a stalker. Also sometimes your emails will end up in a spam filter and no matter how many times you write, you'll never reach that person.

The best way to focus your energy is to write to the person that read your email but didn't reply. How do you do that? If you are in online sales you probably know the answer. There are a couple of free plugins for Gmail and they'll do the job for you.

Personally I use Streak.com by Rewardly a great startup based in San Francisco. I'm not part of this company; I just genuinely love the product. There is a paid version with more advanced customer relationship management, but for a Kickstarter campaign the free version is more than enough. Every time someone reads your email, Streak informs you. If they don't reply to you then you can contact them again in let's say 24-48 hours.

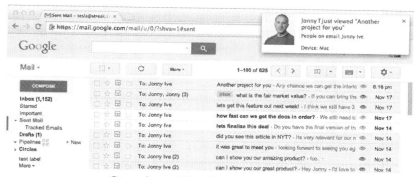

Streak notification and stream

Streak works only with Gmail. If you don't have a Gmail account you should open one specifically for the campaign. With Google Apps for business you can now have a Gmail account ending with your domain name (i.e. not name@gmail.com but name@startupagora.com).

An Alternative: Boomerang.com

Gmail for business is one of the best tools for running

a crowdfunding campaign. Besides Streak or the alternative Boomerang.com (also works with Gmail only) you would use shared documents and shared spreadsheets with your virtual assistant. Every assistant knows how to use Gmail and for a 30 day campaign you don't want to go through time consuming training on other systems.

Just a note: at the time of writing Boomerang requires a monthly subscription if your email is with Google Apps.

Another Alternative: Mailtrack.io

In the last few months I've been a frequent user of Mailtrack.io. It's not a CRM like Streak, in fact it lacks the project management stream that makes Streak such a great app, but sometimes "less is more". The main focus of Mailtrack.io is in its name: it's a mail tracker. Every time someone reads your email a green tick shows in your inbox near the email. It's fast and simple to use.

I love their no-frills approach. I'm sure that they are planning to add more, but still simple to use, features. It will be interesting to follow them.

You can download this free tool online: http:// Mailtrack.io

How to Set Up Pledges That Sell

Early Bird

There are many ways to play a piece. As long as you never play safe.
– SIR MARK ELDER, orchestra conductor

Pick one of your pledges and mirror the same reward at a discounted price but in limited numbers. That's an Early Bird.

Early Birds create a sense of urgency and encourage visitors to turn into backers sooner rather than later. Raising money in the first days of the campaign is essential to be labeled as a winner and acquire even more backers. Not to mention that a fast fund raiser could get you onto the home page of Kickstarter as a featured campaign. Now that's going to bring traffic and funds.

Early Birds also reward those early backers who bet on you before the campaign becomes a clear winner. They deserve it.

Thank You Pledge

Never underestimate the value of a nice surprise.
– MATT HOMANN, The (non)billable hour

Not every backer wants your product; some of them just want to support your campaign. That's why you see so many campaigns with a $1 or $5 Thank You Pledge.

From the very beginning Kickstarter has attracted an assortment of practical dreamers and innovators. Creators are often repeat backers, and vice versa, backers become creators - or want to be in the future. We understand the struggle of a fellow entrepreneur and we want them to succeed. Besides, sooner or later it may be our turn to benefit from this amazing ecosystem.

Which Pledge is Better? $1 or $5?

I would go for the $1 pledge, because you'll attract more backers. If you are a regular communicator or—even better—if you plan to post a series of update videos during the campaign then you can turn many of these supporters into real backers who will purchase your product.

On the contrary, if you are less confident about your

updates or your project, or promote an important social value, you can go for the $5 pledge and cash the money. Personally, I've never done that, but I know many smart veterans who swear that the $5 pledge is better.

Before you set your Thank You Pledge make sure that it's not going to cannibalize your product. For instance if you are selling an app at $1.99 or an eBook at $6.99 it makes no sense to have a Thank You Pledge of $1 or $5 respectively. If someone just wants to support you he will probably purchase the app at $1.99. This means more money and it pushes up the total number of downloads. If you give him the chance to pledge $1 you'll just lose a sale.

True Story: An Innovative Use of the Thank You Pledge by OwnPhones

In any moment of decision the best thing you can do is the right thing, the next best thing is the wrong thing, and the worst thing you can do is nothing.
– THEODORE ROOSEVELT

OwnPhones is–in the words of their creator–"The world's first 3D printed wireless earbuds custom fitted to your ears and perfectly designed to match your personality".

You scan your ear with your smartphone and a state of the art 3D printer produces earbuds completely customised to your ear. That's what happens inside your ear but from an external point of view the earbuds may look like (almost) anything you like, from a minimalistic black plug to a golden skull, and everything in between.

With such unusual and high tech hardware it's no surprise that OwnPhones reached their goal. Actually the initial target was pulverised in the first week, with a final fundraiser of $767,472 - more than 300% of the initial goal.

I'm a backer and when I was looking at the campaign I found their use of the Thank You Pledge very interesting. This pledge is not visible anymore on their Kickstarter page, and I went for another pledge. But the content was more or less something like this:

"In exchange for $5, you'll get the (usual) thank you note and your name in the hall of fame PLUS a $15 discount voucher to purchase OwnPhones when they're available to the public".

That's one of the best pledges I've ever seen. On top of the usual benefits (money and the backer's email) OwnPhones will turn a series of backers into customers at no extra cost to them.

#UPDATE - While chatting with the team at OwnPhones, I received this unfortunate news: "Hi Stefano, Kickstarter notified us that we cannot offer those types of pledges, so we removed the ones that offered vouchers for future purchases."

Nothing wrong with that. When you manage a bold campaign like OwnPhones, you can't succeed everywhere. In fact, if every tactic is successful, you probably haven't been bold enough.

Discount vouchers can't be used on Kickstarter. Nonetheless I've decided to keep this chapter in for two reasons.

1. First, it's useful to know what is forbidden as much as what it works. Thanks to OwnPhones now we know that voucher pledges are forbidden.

2. Second, because it's still a great idea. You can't use vouchers on Kickstarter, but you could still find them useful in other ways. Maybe you decide to use your own platform like Chris Roberts of Star Citizen (more about this in "True Story: Meet the Urban Heroes") or maybe you will use them on your website. No need to limit yourself to one platform.

Campaigns from This Chapter

- OwnPhones: Wireless, Custom-Fit, 3D Printed Earbuds (by Itamar Joban and others) http://kck.st/1p6JuZQ

The Backer Borne Pledge

Grow your favorite clients into your best ones.
Then depend upon your best clients to grow your business.
– MATT HOMANN, The (non)billable hour

Another effective hack to improve your fund raising is to involve backers in the creation of a pledge. You will always receive many suggestions from backers and visitors, or–better–you can make it clear on your page, in your messages or on your social media that you are actively looking for their suggestions. The more you involve prospect backers in the creative project, the higher the chance is you'll turn them into real backers.

The backlash of this hack is that it could be time consuming and chaotic. You'll spend many hours replying to their messages, particularly to manage the proposals that you did NOT deliver. Nobody likes to be asked for advice and be ignored, thus you should contact them on a one-to-one basis, if possible, to explain that their idea was great but you didn't use their idea THIS TIME for reasons of time/expense/etc. You can tell them that your team will reconsider their advice when the product is available to the general public.

You don't have to praise every single idea like that, but remember that they dedicated unpaid time to help your business. Even if it's not the smartest idea that you have ever heard they deserve your respect.

You have to find that delicate balance between involving the community and not losing too much time. It's all part of the game. Start playing and you'll become better at it.

Limited Edition Pledge

Imitation is the sincerest form of flattery.
– CHARLES CALEB COLTON

Every campaign should have one or more limited edition pledge. It could be a limited number of books signed by the author or an exclusive dinner; the only limit is your imagination. If you are not the creative type have a look at similar campaigns, especially successful past campaigns and copy them.

Put the Backer in the Pledge

My greatest fear is not that i set the standard to high and fail to reach it, but that i set it too low and achieve it.
– MICHELANGELO (1475 – 1564)

This one of the most successful pledges on Kickstarter and it's almost free for you. Offer a limited number of backers the chance to be part of your product. If you are an author you can give a character their name or the name of their loved ones. If you are launching a gaming app you can give their face to a minor character (medium pledge), a main character (expensive pledge) or the princess and the hero (very expensive pledge).

This hack has been used a long time before Kickstarter, and when I say "a long time" I really mean that. In the 16th century Michelangelo portrayed many celebrities of his time as angels or saints on the Sistine Chapel in Rome. We don't have prove that he get funded but it's quite possible. If this "pledge" worked for Michelangelo, I'm sure it will work for you.

#TRIVIA – Michelangelo painted the ceiling of the Sistine Chapel working non stop for four years (1508-1512). In the masterpiece, he left at least two self portraits and the faces of many celebrities of his time.

One of the self portraits is hidden in the scene of St Bartholomew holding the skin of a man flayed alive. Ironically, Michelangelo didn't paint his face on the saint but on the tortured man. This is his unconventional way of complaining to his boss—the Pope—about working four years non-stop, without weekends or holidays. On the contrary, one of the "celebrities" is in hell, with donkey ears and a snake biting his genitals. The face is Baigio da Cenesa, the papal master of ceremonies. The cardinal complained to the Pope about the excessive nudity in the painting, demanding a cover up. Not only did Michelangelo ignore the request, but the memory of the cardinal is mocked in front of 25,000 tourists a day. Now that's true revenge!

Stretch Goals

Everything should be made as simple as possible, but not simpler.
– ALBERT EINSTEIN

"A stretch goal is a funding target set by the project creator beyond the original goal." This is the official description of a stretch goal according to the Kickstarter Help Center. The difference between the original goal and the stretch goal(s) is substantial.

1. If you don't reach the **original goal** even by one cent you don't get any funds and Kickstarter will reimburse all the backers at no charge.

Kickstarter supports this aggressive system to protect the backers and their own reputation. The primary goal is the minimum amount of money required to create the product according to the creator. Thus, if the campaign doesn't raise this minimum amount, there is a high risk that the product won't be delivered.

2. On the contrary, the **stretch goal** is a marketing tool that activates a bonus. Funds are collected whether stretch goals are met or not, as long as the project has met its original goal.

For instance, SCiO—a pocket molecular sensor that we'll cover in the next true story—set a stretch goal of $2 million. If this goal was reached (it was) the company would have provided free apps to every backer for two years.

Why the stretch goal is such a great marketing tool

The stretch goal benefits every backer, including the existing one. This is an amazing feature because when the stretch goal is announced, every past backer is transformed into a potential sales manager. If they want to reap the benefits, they have to convince their network to support the campaign as well.

I'm not saying that having a stretch goal is mandatory but you should at least consider it. Have a look at similar campaigns then make your decision.

You can still change your mind in the middle of the campaign. In fact many stretch goals are communicated when the campaign is already up and running.

There Is No Limit to Stretch Goals

You are only required to set one primary goal. But you can set as many stretch goals as you want. In fact, it's very common for a campaign to set up just a stretch goal. When it's reached they then set a second stretch goal, generating new excitement among the backers and new buzz in the media.

What's the Best Time to Set a Stretch Goal?

There is a debate among crowdfunding veterans about the best moment to communicate a stretch goal.

1. Some suggest setting a stretch goal from the beginning, so your backers are encouraged to promote your product from day one.

2. Others maintain the opposite. Setting a stretch goal from the beginning highlights that something is missing in the original pledge. And because at the beginning the stretch goal is far away it will only discourage the backers.

Personally I've seen both strategies work. It really depends on the campaign. But if I had to make a general statement, I would go for setting a stretch goal in the middle of the campaign. This has two positive effects.

First, a stretch goal in the middle of a campaign is more effective. For instance, if you communicate a stretch goal of $1 million when you have already raised $750,000, the goal looks achievable. You "just" need to raise $250,000, a fraction of what you already have done. This is going to energize the backers. On the contrary, if you communicate the same goal from the beginning, it will look far away, and nobody wants to spend his unpaid time if the odds are against him.

Second, a stretch goal in the middle of a campaign is a great opportunity to contact bloggers again. It's a new story, and also a very good one. With just one message you communicate to the journalist that you have reached the goal AND ALSO that there is a new exciting goal. That's probably something worth writing about.

In short, if you communicate a stretch goal at the beginning of the campaign, it should be reachable.

A Stretch Goal Doesn't Have to Be Connected to Funding

Not every stretch goal has to be connected to funding. For instance, a stretch goal based on the number of backers has proven very effective. Especially when it's an alternative to a monetary goal. A great example is the list of goals reported by SCiO, the next true story:

- **Primary goal:** $200,000
- **Stretch goal #1:** 4,000 backers
  (Communicated in the middle of the campaign)
- **Stretch goal #2:** $2 million
  (Communicated in the middle of the campaign after reaching stretch goal #1 and after having already raised the majority of the sum)

True Story: Meet SCiO - Your Sixth Sense

The greatest pleasure in life is doing what people say you cannot do.
– Anonymous

SCiO looks like one of those pocket sensors from Star Trek, but it was actually developed by real engineers after a successful campaign on Kickstarter.

To understand the success of this campaign think about the fact that from an original goal of $200,000 they raised over $2.76 million. That's 1,381% of the target.

I'm not going to write a long story because the majority of the information is in the previous chapter. Stretch goals are not the only reason this campaign was successful. In fact everything was near perfection: a great idea, a great video, an impressive team, and constant media contact. I suggest studying SCiO's entire page and their website.

This is a great case study for stretch goals. The first stretch goal (4,000 backers) generated many $1 pledges through the consequential viral effect. The second stretch goal ($2 million, thus 1,000% of the original goal) has been used to pitch to the media.

#TRIVIA - The most successful campaigns on Kickstarter last for 4 days. SCiO is the exception to the rule. The campaign is one of the longest in the history of Kickstarter, lasting from 29 April to 15 June. A 47 day long campaign. I'm sure that raising $2.76 million was a great paycheck for all the effort.

Campaigns from This Chapter

- SCiO: Your Sixth Sense. A Pocket Molecular Sensor For All (by Consumer Physics, Inc.) http://kck.st/1hPqZ6I

8 Things to Do at the Beginning of Your Campaign

1. Best Duration for Your Campaign

Nine women can't make a baby in a month.
– MARK SUSTER, Serial Entrepreneur and Venture Capitalist

At this point, your project has been accepted by Kickstarter, and you need to decide upon the length of your campaign. In theory, you can pick any life span from 1 day to 60 days, however the most successful campaigns are one month long.

#TIP - The most successful campaigns on Kickstarter are 30 days long.

We all fantasise about raising more money using the entire time frame of 60 days, but this could be a huge mistake. Every expert salesman knows that he has a better chance of closing a deal if he instills a sense of urgency in the buyer. This is true for crowdfunding as well.

Kickstarter proved this theory changing their Terms of Service after two years of experimenting. Until 2011 campaigns were allowed to last up to 90 days, but this option was removed due to poor performance. Only 24% of the long campaigns were successful; a nice way of saying that 3 out of 4 were a complete failure. On the contrary, the overall success of the shorter campaigns was almost double.

Look at the graph "Project Duration vs. Success Rate" created by Kickstarter; it's quite convincing.

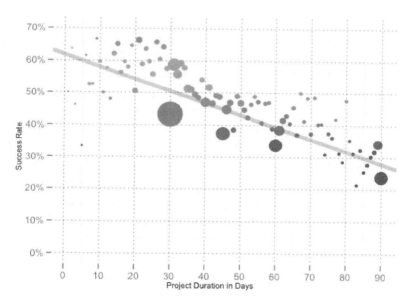

Campaign duration vs. Success rate (Source: Kickstarter)

The Exception to the Rule

When a campaign needs to raise a limited amount of money, for instance $5,000, I've seen a high ratio of success with a length of 3 weeks. This is especially true for small campaigns who aim to finance books and comics as it is likely that the backers won't want to wait too long to read the end product.

It's possible that your campaign could work better using the entire time frame of 60 days, although I doubt it. Feel free to pick a different length, if you truly feel that you are an exception to the rule. After all, making exceptions to the rule is what makes great entrepreneurs. You know what they say:

The bad entrepreneur ignores the rules. The good entrepreneur knows the rules. The great entrepreneur learns the rules to understand which ones to break.

2. Best Time of the Year to Start a Campaign

Don't wait for the perfect moment.
Take the moment and make it perfect.
– Old saying

There are never-ending discussions among Kickstarter veterans regarding the best time of year to start a campaign. Personally, the only rule I believe in is "not during the holidays".

1. About Launching during the Holidays

Not surprisingly people tend to use Facebook and the internet mostly at work, and not during their lunch break. This alone could start an interesting discussion about when and why corporate jobs became so boring, but this is a discussion for another day.

In short, don't start a campaign at Christmas, in the middle of summer, or during any other major holiday. And don't forget to check the calendars of other countries (Google Calendar has a database for almost every country on earth). For example, if you hope to have backers in the United States, don't start a campaign on the 4th of July.

True, there have been some exceptions, with a few successful campaigns working during these periods. However I wonder if the campaigns would have been even more successful if their owners had picked a different time.

2. About Finding the Best Month of the Year

As for the exact month, most entrepreneurs say that March and September are best although not everybody agrees. Personally I don't care too much. My personal quote on the subject is "Don't wait for the perfect moment. Take the moment and make it perfect".

If your team is ready don't wait too long or you'll lose the momentum. Excitement has won many more campaigns than cold hard planning.

True Story: Meet Ryan Grepper and his Coolest Cooler

Anyone who has never made a mistake has never tried anything new.
– ALBERT EINSTEIN

I don't care too much about the month of the campaign. If your team is ready, start your project before their excitement fades. Passion wins more battles than planning.

There is always an exception though.

Ryan Grepper is the creator of the biggest Kickstarter project ever. His cooler raised over $13.2 million or 26,570% of his goal. Even more interestingly, Ryan failed on Kickstarter the first time round.

The Coolest, a gadget packed cooler with built-in blender, music speakers and USB charger, was a complete failure . . . the first time. In the second campaign Ryan improved his video and the design. You can compare them by having a look at the campaign links below. He improved his pitch to the media, and got the support of the community who backed his first campaign.

Besides all these improvements, Ryan candidly

admits that the biggest mistake of the first campaign was the timing. He launched the first campaign in November, with closing and shipping from December; not really the best time of the year to purchase a cooler.

This true story sends me back to the initial question: what is Kickstarter? It's not a place to invest in companies. It's a pre-sales platform. As an investor I would have liked the project the first time round. I can invest in a company even if I have to wait a few months for the summer. However on Kickstarter I don't get equity (company shares). I get a cooler. And I don't need a cooler in December, well not in the US or North Europe at least.

From a personal point of view I owe Ryan one. At the time of writing we are discussing about a project for a 3D printed mini racing car. A cool toy that you can personalise at zero cost and drive with your smartphone. After studying the Coolest Cooler campaign we'll probably wait until Christmas. Thanks Ryan, you deserve your $13 million!

Campaigns from This Chapter

- The Coolest Cooler (by Ryan Greeper)
  First campaign (unsuccessful):
  http://kck.st/1hfaWUu
  Second campaign:

http://kck.st/1oweGkH

3. Best Day of the Week to Start a Campaign

Whether you think you can, or you think you can't - you are tight.
– HENRY FORD

I receive this question quite often but I don't think the day of the week is so important, unless it's the weekend. The weekend is bad for the same reason why it's bad to launch during the holidays: people surf the internet mostly at work.

This is not true if you have a special event during the weekend: a concert, a TV interview, or anything else that gives you a stage. In this case it's probably worth launching during the event.

Besides that, I tend to activate campaigns during the night between Sunday and Monday. On a Monday morning a nice video on Kickstarter could brighten the day of millions of frustrated employees. Their boss will not love you but for many others you will look like a kind of hero.

4. Set Up Free Stats for Your Campaign

You must track it or it didn't happen.
– NOAH KAGAN, founder Appsumo

Bitly.com is one of the most popular link shortening services used by many including–guess who?– Kickstarter. The immediate result is that if you add a "+" to the end of the URL of your project you'll get access to amazing stats about your campaign.

Best of all it's free.

This Is How You Access the Free Stats

Once you publish your campaign you will get a dedicated short URL. You can find this short URL for every campaign by clicking the embed button under the video.

Click this button and copy the short link on the right bottom corner. I've added an example from Amanda Palmer's campaign, the most successful music project on Kickstarter, with over £1 million dollars raised in just one month.

A Step by Step Guide

In case you love simple step by step instructions like me here is a guide.

1.   Click the embed button
2.   Copy the short link (e.g. http://kck.st/JliwH9)
3.   Paste the short link into your browser adding a + at the end (e.g.: http://kck.st/JliwH9+).
4.   If you don't have a Bitly account the browser will request you create one at this point. Accept it. It's free.
5.   Enjoy the free stats.
6.   Save the link to your bookmarks and check it regularly.
7.   It's a good idea to follow the same process for campaigns similar to yours. For instance, if you see a specific social media platform being particularly effective for another campaign, you can reconsider your strategy. Or you can find a blogger very active about a product similar to yours and contact him, and so on.

Step by Step Screenshots

Step 1: click the embed button under the video

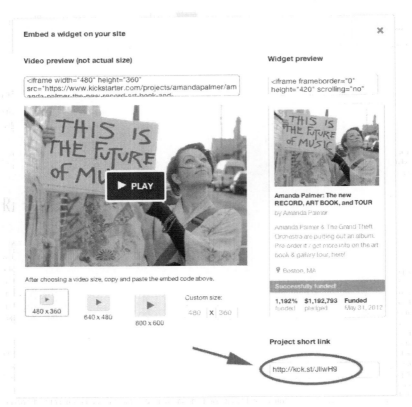

Step 2 : Copy the short link (http://kck.st/JliwH9)

Step 3 : Paste the short link into your browser adding a "+" at the end. Enjoy the free stats! (Image source for the entire process: Amanda Palmer Kickstarter page)

5. Get Informed if a Blogger Talks About You (Hint: Not Google Alarm)

> *When you innovate, you've got to be prepared for people telling you that you are nuts.*
> *– LARRY ELLISON, Co-founder of Oracle*

Every time a blogger or anybody else talks about your campaign, you want to be immediately informed.

1. You can thank the author in the comment area of his post. First of all because he deserves your gratitude—no matter how small or big his blog is—he's promoting your product free of charge. Second because you'll have a record of your name and a commitment to every person who read the post.

2. Eventually, if the blog is big enough or you like the blogger, you can establish a long term relationship with him (or her). He has already written about your product, he's already interested in you, thus building a relationship should be relatively easy. Building such relationships is not useful just for this Kickstarter campaign—the blogger can tweet

and post updates about your campaign—it's a long term investment. Your job doesn't stop with the end of Kickstarter; on the contrary the campaign end is the start of your job as a "normal" entrepreneur. I know that I've already said that, but it's an important point that many tend to underestimate, including a younger version of myself.

There are many free services providing these updates. Personally I use Talkwalker Alerts and I know many online experts—including SEO experts—strongly advocating this website. I don't have shares in this Luxembourg based startup, I just like their services.

Talkwalker provides many searches and analytics—eventually you want to have a look at their main website Talkwalker.com—but in this paragraph I'm speaking just about their alert. You plug in a keyword such as the name of your product and they create a news alarm. You get an email (almost) every time someone enters this word on the Web.

This is not the only service, I'm sure there are other good competitors. If you think that one service is particularly good I would love to hear from you. My updated contacts details are on http://startupagora.com/help

What Type of News Alarm to Set Up?

That's a good question. Ideally you want to be kept informed on a daily basis about your campaign, but not be overwhelmed by too many emails. Most of the time I usually set up the following alarms:

1. The name of the product (of course);
2. The name of the company;
3. The name of the team members. This can sometimes be a pain, for instance there is a band who play–I think–Italian country music where the name of one artist is Stefano and the surname of another one is Tresca. Since I've a permanent alarm on Talkwalker with my entire name "Stefano Tresca" I get regular updates about all their dates. One day I should buy a ticket for one of their concerts.

6. Beta Test Your Product Online

Do not fear going forward slowly; fear only to stand still.
– Chinese Proverb

This tool is not for everybody but it's quite useful if your Kickstarter is about a book or any other product with a main image. If you are running one of those campaigns the chances are that your designer has already sent you many alternative versions of the image. You like 2-3 of them but you can't be sure which will be best in the eyes of the customers. (If you don't have any doubt, you are a lucky man. I have this feeling all the time.)

One solution is to let the customers decide. Pick the 2-3 images you like the most and use a survey website like PickFu (http://bit.ly/pickf) to create a pool in two minutes and allow complete strangers to vote for the best image.

You can use any website; Pickfu is just the one I've used in the past. The idea is to get impartial feedback outside your circle of friends because your friends say what you want to hear, not what you need to hear. What's good for your pride, it's usually bad for business.

7. Checklist for Your Kickstarter Page

Customers don't measure you on how hard you tried. They measure you on what you deliver.
— STEVE JOBS

Every business needs to sell much more than their product. They promote the brand, the user experience, and everything in between. On Kickstarter this necessity reaches its ultimate level because there is no product at all. Your page is the best place to compensate for this gap, a place where you can promote that "everything else" beyond the product.

Here is a check list of must-do's that we use to develop the page. If you have anything to add, contact me. I always appreciate a good tip.

Kickstarter Page Checklist

❑ Who is behind the campaign?

Speak about you, your motivation and introduce your team. Explain why you the right person to bring this project to life.

❏ What will be the end product? What unique benefit will it provide?

❏ Who is your typical backer? Why should they be interested?

❏ When will the backers receive their pledge?

This information should be very clear.

❏ Do you have a good mix of pledges?

❏ How are you going to spend the money?

❏ What will happen if you exceed your goal?

Many creators promise extra features or faster development if the campaign reaches a higher goal. More about stretch goals in the Pledge chapter.

❏ Do you have a compelling video?

See the chapter "13 Hacks to Make a Successful Video for Kickstarter"

Other Elements You Might Want to Define

❏ Will you accept backers outside your country?

This is especially useful for physical products.

8. Get the Best Consultants for Free

Only those who are asleep make no mistakes.
– INGVAR KAMPRAD, Founder of Ikea

One of the best consultants for Kickstarter is – of course – Kickstarter. The company has an amazing team of experts in different fields who are checking products and campaigns every day. They decide if your project should be featured on the home page or included in the newsletter. Thanks to their job they have seen more projects than any other person on the planet, and they are well aware of what's usually successful and what's not.

The good news is that you can contact them, and get feedback about your project. You can start with the contact page at www.kickstarter.com/contact, eventually you will find the proper dedicated email during the conversation. For instance, if you have a question about design the email is probably technology@kickstarter.com.

I have a few personal email addresses in my contacts but I'm not going to share them in this book. Besides the matter of privacy, people change jobs even in a cool company such as Kickstarter, and the person in charge of a specific area may be someone different by the time you read this book. Not to worry. After sending an initial message through the contact page you usually get a reply from a real manager with specific experience in your area, not a generic call center outside the country. In a busy week you may need to send a second message or a tweet to get their attention, but as a general rule the service is good. And don't forget that it's free.

#TIP – In theory, you can contact the Kickstarter team any moment. However the last thing you want to do is to spam with too many question the person that can put your project in front of 12 million monthly unique visitors. Personally, what I prefer is to finalise the page till the last details, video and cool pictures, and then ask my questions. With a bit of luck, they will not only reply their answer, but our project may be taken note of. I can't say that you win the home page or the newsletter every time, but you definitively increase your chance. Moreover, if you can move a spike of traffic during the first day/week trough the tactics analysed in the marketing and media chapters, they already know you. It's a long shoot, but that's worth trying.

12 Marketing Hacks for Your Campaign

1. Send Them One Sock

Entrepreneurs do more than anyone thinks possible with less than anyone thinks possible.
– JOHN DOERR, early backer of Google and Amazon

"Send them One Sock" is an old marketing quote, yet it still works. The concept is simple. If a product can be divided into parts, you can promote it by providing the first share for free–i.e. book one of a trilogy, or the first episode of a show.

On Kickstarter it works even better than usual. In fact, a backer's main concern is that you are never going to deliver. The common perception of crowdfunding is that there are plenty of great ideas–especially games and hardware–which have been funded but never produced. Delays are becoming a painfully regular issue in crowdfunding. By the very nature of Kickstarter, the project creators are usually single people or small companies, and the backer can't get a reimbursement like he would if he bought a defective product from a major corporation.

That's why giving away part of your product for free could be your best marketing tool. People will download the product–just because it's free–and eventually be interested in the follow up. If you think that this is a tactic for small desperate companies, just have a look at iTunes. Almost every successful TV show provides the pilot free of charge.

Giving a free sample away is effective in itself, but in crowdfunding it is much more than that. It's proof that you have the skills to make the product. This is not obvious. If a major company launches a new product, everybody takes it for granted that the product will work, even when it's not successful (anybody old enough to remember the Zune?) The same rule doesn't apply to you.

Sure this tactic can't be used for every campaign–you can't ship 20% of a Pebble watch–but when it can be used (a book, a comic, a movie in episodes) it gives you an advantage over the other campaigns in your area.

This marketing tactic is particularly useful for newbies, but it can be effective for anybody. I'll give you an example. One of the most exciting projects I've consulted on is a 6 episode movie set in the universe of Metal Gear Solid. The creators don't need to prove their pedigree, in fact they already released a successful first Metal Gear Solid movie in 2009. Since then they have amassed downloads, fans and even the praise of the author of Metal Gear Solid, Hideo Kojima himself. Despite their existing fame, the first episode of the new movie is free for everybody, not just the backers. There are two main reasons for that, both listed in the next case study.

True Story: Metal Gear Solid, the Movie

The best way to predict the future is to invent it.
– ALAN KAY

The name of the team is Hive Division. These talented video makers built their reputation through their first movie in 2009, set in the same Metal Gear universe. So why are they sharing a free episode years later?

We are not speaking about a low cost amateur production here, but a real movie with special effects, from people that are usually paid by big corporations to make commercials. There are two main reasons:

1. The first and most obvious reason is that skills and technology have advanced massively since 2009. The first movie still regularly gets downloaded thousands of times but it now doesn't look as good as a modern professional movie.

2. More importantly: bloggers love to talk about high quality free stuff. A movie about something popular like Metal Gear Solid will easily be promoted by the major online magazines. In crowdfunding, the best strategies

are usually "bottom to top": starting from small blogs and moving up the chain later. However if you can share a high quality product for free, you are the exception to the rule. You can aim for the top journalists from day one.

Campaigns from This Chapter

You can find the first movie "MGS Philanthropy" free here:

http://bit.ly/mgs-p

The new movie is a work in progress the time of writing. If you drop me your email (http://startupagora.com/register) or connect with me on Twitter (http://twitter.com/startupagora) I'll let you know as soon as it's online.

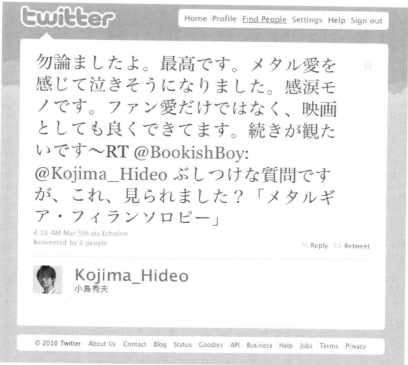

勿論ましたよ。最高です。メタル愛を
感じて泣きそうになりました。感涙モ
ノです。ファン愛だけではなく、映画
としても良くできてます。続きが観た
いです～RT @BookishBoy:
@Kojima_Hideo ぶしつけな質問です
が、これ、見られました？「メタルギ
ア・フィランソロピー」

4.10 AM Mar 5th via Echofon
Retweeted by 6 people

Reply ⟲ Retweet

Kojima_Hideo
小島秀夫

© 2010 Twitter   About Us   Contact   Blog   Status   Goodies   API   Business   Help   Jobs   Terms   Privacy

A fan asks Kojima Hideo–creator of Metal Gear Solid–about the first movie made by Hive Division. "I know this must be asking too much, but did you see MGS Philanthropy?" "Of course I did. It's awesome. I felt like crying for their love for Metal Gear. It's also a well made movie. I can't wait to see the next part."

2. Sharing Pics on Imgur

If Plan A fails, remember that you have 25 letters left.
– Anonymous

I would be surprised if you have never used Imgur.com "the simple image sharer". This website is so popular that in 2014 they raised a $40 million investment from Andreessen Horowitz, the venture capital backed by the founders of Netscape (by the way, THIS is a software I could believe you have never used if you are under 30).

Imgur is popular and it is free. Strangely enough, many marketing consultants ignore this website, focusing their entire campaign on Google Adwords and–recently–Facebook ads. Their problem is budget v. creativity, I guess. They have the money to buy ads, but not necessarily the creativity to develop interesting or funny images. The open voting system at Imgur prevents any lousy images from reaching the home page, no matter how much you pay. In fact, on Imgur you can't pay at all (or–to be accurate–you can't pay "yet". We'll see what happens. Mark Zuckerberg has prevented any form of ads on Facebook for a long time).

Imgur is not a place to upload self promotional ads

however it can be a massive marketing tool for your Kickstarter campaign. The trick to maximizing Imgur is to produce an image that is both interesting for the viewer AND in keeping with your campaign. It's not simple, I know, but it can be incredibly rewarding. It's definitively simpler if your product is related to fantasy, sci-fi or entertainment. Have a look at how "The Seed", a successfully funded game on Kickstarter, used Imgur.

True Story: The Seed by Misery Dev.

We can't solve problems by using the same kind of thinking we used when we created them.
– ALBERT EINSTEIN

The Seed is a "story-driven post-apocalyptic video game set in Eastern Europe in 2016" and I'm proud to be a backer. I don't play online much anymore but the idea and the design was so compelling that I wanted to see this campaign succeed anyway.

Besides, Nicolai Aaroe–the Danish leader of the development team–made a killing on Imgur, reaching more than 124,000 views in a couple of days – all for no cost. The first and most popular image was a sort of "Photoshop your city so it looks like a zombie apocalypse has taken place" how-to. (Zombie is my addition, there are no undead in the game. But don't worry: it's got plenty of mutants, scavengers and action).

You can have a look at the stats below and at the original image online: http://imgur.com/gallery/bhQnl9G. You'll notice that there is no trace of self promotion in the image. The design is beautiful, the idea of the how-to is brilliant and—most importantly—it's in keeping with the game. They didn't just upload a generic, nice design which would have attracted the wrong type of viewer; they made a specific apocalypse scenario. Whoever liked this photo had a good chance of becoming a backer.

With almost no marketing costs, The Seed raised 139% of its goal in one of the toughest areas on Kickstarter: gaming. Indeed many games have been financed through crowdfunding, but it's becoming increasingly difficult if you don't have a famous developer or other star player on your team. And yet they did it. Cheers!

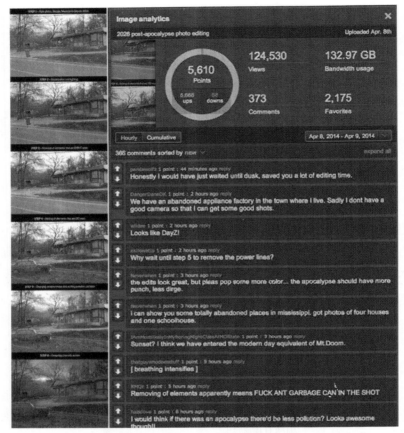

"2026 post-apocalypse photo editing" by The Seed. Imgur analytics.

Campaigns from This Chapter

- The Seed (by Misery Dev. Ltd and Nicolai Aaroe) http://kck.st/1mfsx19

3. One Thousand Tweets Tactic

Human nature has a tendency to admire complexity but to reward simplicity.
– BEN HUH, Founder of Cheezburger

The name of this tool is Thunderclap (http://bit.ly/ thunderclapLink) and it has been used to promote every kind of campaign, from our case study "Shadow" to The White House. Yes, even President Obama has used Thunderclap, as well as stars like Beyonce, and private companies like Mozilla.

Thunderclap is an "online flash mob". You invite your network to join a thunderclap and their social media accounts will share the same message at the same time. Moving the concept to crowdfunding, it means that your entire network of friends and contacts can book a tweet in advance, and all the messages will be sent at the same very moment.

This online flash mob has a double effect:

1. It promotes your project to the "normal" crowd. It's more difficult to ignore a link if many of your friends are talking about it at the same time.
2. It makes it easier to contact bloggers. If you

contact them just after the thunderclap, they'll see that there is interest in your campaign.

Thunderclap started as a Twitter tool, but it now includes Facebook and Tumblr. It can't save a bad campaign by itself, but it can definitely help a good campaign to succeed. Consider Thunderclap for what is: one of your many tools.

True Story: Meet Jean Bey and Prodigy

We can't be afraid to be weird.
– ANDREW MASON, Founder of Groupon

Prodigy is one of the successful campaigns that took advantage of Thunderclap. But this is not just a story about Thunderclap. This team from Paris, lead by the talented Jean Bey, did much more than that.

Prodigy is a card game that uses high quality fantasy figurines (miniatures) and hardware. Card games usually don't perform particularly well on Kickstarter, miniatures perform better, and so does some of the hardware. Prodigy has them all, plus–being based on a fantasy game–they have built a good and growing community; another strong element of success. Not surprisingly Prodigy reached their target, raising 212% of their goal, and they are still selling online after the campaign ended.

Thunderclap is not the only tactic they used. Their success started when they created the right product. Don't focus just on their use of Thunderclap, have a look at the entire campaign, and check out the use of images in the updates. The entire campaign is a learning experience.

Campaigns from This Chapter

- Prodigy the Game (by Hanakai Studio and Jean Bey)
  http://kck.st/1lnbPdu

4. Get the Stars on Your Side

*Because the majority of people out there
are afraid to be different, it allows people
like us to own the ball game.*
*– PETER SHANKMAN, Investor and
Founder of HARO*

Get the stars on your side, or at least one. I'm not talking astronomy here but celebrities. Engaging a celebrity is one of the most well known tactics, one of the most desired but also one of the least used.

I admit it's very hard to get a star on your project free of charge. It's easier, but still challenging, if you are running a social project, and very difficult for anybody else. Still, it's not impossible. Spending one hour brain storming with your team every week could be a great investment.

It can't be a random spray and pray; the goal is to find someone connected to your project. For instance The Great Kingdom—a documentary about the creation of Dungeons & Dragons—got Ernest Gary Gygax Jr., involved. He's the son of the creator of Dungeons & Dragons and very much involved in the role game and fantasy arena.

One of the Kickstarter movies I've backed, "Star

Trek: Axnar" got support from George Takei, the popular actor who plays Hikaru Sulu, helmsman of the original USS Enterprise.

True Story: Star Trek Axanar and George Takei

If you can micromanage someone, he's probably not an A player.
- GUY KAWASAKI

It's unlikely that your campaign attracts someone as popular as George Takei. He's not just an actor; he's a legend and an activist with hundreds of thousands of followers on social media. However, you don't need to find the most famous celebrity; your goal is to find someone who may have a specific interest in your project (besides you never know how far you can go until you try). Whoever you attract, the following is an example of a well played out engagement. The team behind Star Trek Axnar didn't brag about having such a great testimonial. They engaged him with some humor.

1. George Takei posts his message on Facebook.

George Takei shared a link via Crowd Powered.
12 hours ago · Edited

One of the reasons I follow "Crowd Powered"--always find innovative and exciting projects. Trekkies, you don't want to miss this. Quite impressive. Truly. Be sure to click on the kickstarter link and lend a hand to help make the whole production happen. Less than a day to go.

Star Trek: Axanar

"Axanar" is the story of Garth of Izar & the Battle of Axanar, a pivotal event in the history of the Federation.

Like · Comment · Share   5,231 Shares

Robert Meyer Burnett, Diana Kingsbury, Ryan T Husk and 10,805   Top Comments ▾
others like this.

George Takei's original post on Facebook

2. The Axanar team replies directly on Kickstarter.

The team's reply

#TIP – Start Trek Axanar, Veronica Mars and Soma are just three examples of campaigns using the update section of Kickstarter as a blog. At the very beginning, this section was created to update the backers about product development, nothing else. However, over the last few years it has become a powerful tool for creating a community. Basically it's like having a blog with paying users. Only paying customers (the backers) can access the news, and the technology is provided by Kickstarter free of charge. A few practical tips:

i) Don't wait until end of the campaign to start using the updates

ii) Don't use this section just to brag about being published by an online magazine

iii) Do use this section to create a conversation instead. Post a photo of your team working on the project, ask the backers what they think about new ideas, etc. In short, empower your community.

Campaigns from This Chapter

- Start Trek: Axanar (by Axanar Production and Alex Peters)
  http://kck.st/1xc0Bwr

5. Find Your Tribe

Call it a clan, call it a network, call it a tribe, call it a family: Whatever you call it, whoever you are, you need one.
– JANE HOWARD

This is not a chapter about building "your own community"; that takes too much time to be useful on Kickstarter. A few project creators such as Minaal are capable of growing their community during a campaign but they are the exception to the rule.

One the contrary, this is a chapter about using "existing communities" to promote your project.

You are involved in communities in your "normal" life and now you would probably like to see how they work in a crowdfunding environment. This is exactly what we are going to look at in the following true story.

True Story: Meet the Urban Heroes

Success in startup is like being pregnant. Everyone congratulates you. But no one knows how many times you were f*cked before you got there.
– Anonymous

Urban Heroes isn't the biggest campaign out there but it's a great case study due to their capacity to succeed against all odds. To be honest, when I first saw this project I thought it had every chance of failing:

1. The product is a new role playing game, one of the lower performing categories on Kickstarter. And I'm not talking about an easy board game but a real role playing game with a thick manual.

2. The team is new with no history of previous success, at least at an international level. Crowdfunding for gaming can be very tough unless you have a well known face on your team. To give you an idea, Chris Roberts–creator of the famous Wing Commander– launched a crowdfunding campaign for a new space game "Start Citizen". Result: $54 million raised. That

isn't a typo, it's fifty four million. With a great idea, great team and . . . his great name, Chris was so confident of getting media coverage and an enormous amount of money that he decided to skip Kickstarter in favour of his own platform. Basically he has a crowdfunding website entirely dedicated to his project. On the contrary, when a team doesn't include any famous names, raising money for a game is extremely hard and many campaigns fail to meet their goal.

3. The team is based in a country with no major usage of Kickstarter (in this case Italy) and none of them have English as their mother tongue. True, Kickstarter has no nationality and you can find backers outside your country. But backers tend to support projects that have already reached at least 40% of their goal. Having a network of contacts in a country with major usage of Kickstarter–i.e. the USA or UK–can speed up the initial dramatic phase of your campaign.

Chances are that you are going to be in a position very similar to Alessandro and Matteo–the two creators of Urban Heroes– without a big name such as Chris Roberts on your team. And yet they succeeded. I've seen these two creators taking part in every conceivable event connected to role playing games, comics or cosplay, not to mention every forum and Facebook page.

There is a quote from Pat Flynn, a master blogger

from Texas: to succeed you should "be every everywhere". In a 30 day crowdfunding campaign you can't disperse your energy, but you can find your peers– your "tribe"–and be present 24/7.

It works best for some types of campaign. A role playing game about super heroes can be promoted at comic fairs, forums and in many pre-existing communities; you can't hope to have such a high number of regular events if your campaign is in a more traditional market. Still, there is a tribe for everything; you just need to find it.

Be prepared, this mix of online forums and offline events is exhausting. I've a great respect for any team that can survive such 24/7 activity for a couple of months. If you are one of them send me a tweet or an email. I'd like to read your story and add it to the book or feature it elsewhere.

Another bizarre idea from the campaign: a magazine for super heroes.

Campaigns from This Chapter

- Urban Heroes (by Tin Hat Games)
  http://kck.st/PweJ4N

6. Twitter Marketing for Crowdfunding

Twitter is the only true social network. Facebook, Pinterest, Tumblr, Instagram have defaulted into content platforms. Twitter is still the one place you can jump into a conversation and nobody thinks it's creepy.
– GARY VAYNERCHUK

There is only one major rule when it comes to tweeting for crowdfunding: "Don't promote yourself". Period! Nobody wants to read an endless stream of tweets glorifying your qualities. We both know that yet the impulse to tweet about our achievements is hard to stop.

If you are into statistics, Guy Kawasaki–former Apple evangelist and author of an incredible number of business books–recommends self promotion for one out of every twenty messages.

Besides using Twitter to engage journalists there are three best practices to use to promote your campaign.

1. Don't promote yourself (see above)
2. Use collateral tweets

3. Use Twitter search properly

That's all. They are simple, extremely time consuming, and you can't avoid them. Or maybe you can, but that means that you are going to campaign without some of the best free weapons out there.

Don't look at me; I'm not the biggest social media user out there. I'm sure you can do much better. My attitude changes when I'm not using the social media for me but for a startup. The commitment that is required can be a pain (it is for me), but I believe it's a small price to pay.

7. The Collateral Twitter Tactic

If you aren't getting rejected on a daily basis, your goals aren't ambitious enough.
– CHRIS DIXON, Co-founder of Hunch and Venture Capitalist

I admit I rarely use this practice for my personal profile. I love to follow my Twitter stream as way to keep updated, but I'm not the most active tweeter out there. This attitude changes completely when I work with a startup or a crowdfunding campaign. Twitter can be the most powerful weapon in your arsenal.

The first and easiest way to use Twitter is . . . sending out tweets. It seems obvious but we'll see over the next few pages that this is not necessarily the most effective strategy.

If the main rule is "don't promote yourself" then what are we going to tweet about? I'm sure you know the answer. Think what your potential customers like. That's usually what YOU like by the way. It's hard to spend hours every day on Twitter messaging about something that you don't care about.

An example. If you are launching a fantasy game app

on Kickstarter, you don't need to write about apps. You might want to tweet fantasy images, updates about Games of Thrones, comics and cosplay. Anything connected to your audience. If they like it, and you like it, they will follow you.

This is sometimes called the "Collateral Twitter" tactic. Back to the example; if you are launching a fantasy gaming app, you have an impulse to tweet about "your app" and about "apps" in general. You tweet fantasy news and pictures instead. You'll get followers interested in fantasy with the possible collateral effect that they'll buy your app.

Then, from time to time you update your followers about your campaign. I should stress the words "then" and "from time to time".

The motto is "Be engaging and they will come".

8. Promote Your Campaign through Twitter Search

Twitter search is imperative.
– GARY VAYNERCHUK

Twitter search is one of the best tools to promote your campaign, and it's free. The process is really simple, and yet the execution takes quite some time.

Go to Twitter Search (http://twitter.com/search) and search the hashtags most connected to your campaign's passions. I need to stress the word "passion". They are not product hashtags but passion hashtags. So, if you are launching a fantasy game app, the hashtag is not #app or #ios, but possibly #LordOfTheRings or #GameOfThrones.

Find people with the same passions and engage them. That's it. There is no secret strategy, nor any sophisticated tactic. Just find people with the same passions, and connect with them.

If the theory is easy, the execution is a completely different matter. I haven't yet found a startupper with the time commitment and the talent to be the best at this game. Engaging on Twitter is time consuming, and it can be very frustrating, especially if you are a tech person not particularly used to sales and networking.

Yet, no matter how shy or geeky the founder of the startup was, I've seen this tactic bring results every time. Indeed, a social media expert might be more effective, but every type of project creator has achieved more results engaging on Twitter than with the majority of the other tools. In my experience, only emailing friends and connections performs better.

You just need to tolerate the frustration of the first few days, when you are not used to the tool and everybody seems to be ignoring you (or worse). I'm not saying that it's simple though.

Go Pro with the Hashtag Search

If you want to try a more advanced hashtag search, have a look at Cybranding (http://cybranding.com) and its free cousin Hashtagify (http://hashtagify.me).

They are not an alternative to Twitter Search. The latter is still the best way to quickly find who's talking about the same passions and contacting them. Cybranding and Hashtagify's strong points are finding related hashtags (for instance, you know that your potential customers like #GamesOfThrones, but what else do they tweet about?), and the trending hashtags for your specific campaigns and the most influential Twitter users not in general, but for your specific goal.

Disclaimer: I'm an investor and an advisor in Cybranding, the company behind these two services. A few months ago, I would have been hesitant to speak about them, to avoid any conflict of interest. But after the launch of the new service, they have been reviewed by over one hundred bloggers and journalists including Wired and Socialmedia Today. They are winning their own spotlight and I'm proud of them.

9. How to Get Free (Real) Retweets

The best time to plant a tree is 20 years ago.
The second best moment is now.
– Chinese Proverb

I'm not talking about buying fake followers here, but about finding real Twitter accounts genuinely interested in Kickstarter. Crowdfunding has become such a hot topic in the last few years that you can find many accounts dedicated to the subject by doing some simple research on Twitter Search (http://twitter.com/search).

In the meantime, I have drawn up an initial list to give you a little competitive advantage. Some of these profiles may retweet your projects, others accept press releases and others are journalists specializing in crowdfunding. The usual rule applies: don't spam them. Read what they have to say before engaging them.

This is an activity that you can start doing at the very beginning before your campaign is online.

#CALL TO ACTION – If you have an account dedicated to crowdfunding, and you don't see it on the list, contact me. We'll decide together whether or not to add your Twitter account to the list.

The popularity of Twitter accounts come and go and this is not an exhaustive list of profiles.

1. **Crowd Funding Forum** @CrowdFundingBB
2. **CrowdFundingPlanning** @CrwdFndPlanning
3. **Best of Kickstarter** @BestKickstarter
4. **GrowthFunders** @growthfunders
5. **CrowdFund Buzz** @icrowdfundbuzz
6. **Ayudos .com** @_ayudos
7. **Crowdfunding** @Crowdfundingx
8. **Kickstarter Forum** @kickstartforum
9. **CrowdFundingBro** @CrowdFundingBro
10. **CrowdFundingPro** @CrowdFundingPro
11. **The Crowdfund Mafia** @CrowdfundMAFIA
12. **Team Crowdfunding** @TeamCrowdfund
13. **Crowdfund Retweeter** @Crowdfund_RT
14. **CrowdSifter** @CrowdSifter

10. Promote Kickstarter Before Kickstarter

When you're forced to be simple, you're forced to face the real problem.
– PAUL GRAHAM, Co-founder of Y Combinator

Crowdfunding has become so popular that many backers would like to know in advance about any campaigns in their area of interest. This way, they can plan their budget and they don't risk missing a campaign. Or maybe they are just curious about what's going on in the market.

To meet these requests websites like Prefundia (http://bit.ly/prefundia) inform backers about any "coming soon". They have an online showcase and–more important–a massive newsletter.

You can upload your campaign to Prefundia before it's completely ready. Many visitors to this website are regular backers and eventually some will convert to be your backers. The online showcase is free, while Prefundia charges a fee if you want to be featured in their newsletter.

At the time of writing, we have only used Prefundia

for one campaign, and I plan to test them out with a few other projects before writing a complete analysis. Anyway it's free, it takes just a couple of minutes to set your showcase up, and it's growing. So you should probably have a look at it.

11. Kickstarter as a Marketing Tool

Every no gets me closer to a yes.
– MARC CUBAN, serial entrepreneur

More proof that crowdfunding has become incredibly popular is the use of Kickstarter and its cousin Indiegogo, which is a marketing tool in itself. It's easier to promote a page on Kickstarter than the generic message: "we are looking for funds".

Backers and even normal customers are used to the look of a Kickstarter page, and they can click more easily on the link of a campaign than a link to an unknown blog. It happens to me as well. I've noticed that every week I tweet one or two campaigns that I find interesting while browsing Kickstarter. For them it's free promotion. I would have never found their product if they were not on Kickstarter or Indiegogo.

To enjoy this promotion, some apply to Kickstarter even if they think that they don't have much chance of succeeding. Even if they don't reach their goal, they have enjoyed extra promotion for 30 days, and they can contact the backers through the platform.

I would not go so far. A failed project on Kickstarter

could damage your brand more than the benefits of the extra promotion. Moreover, if many projects use these platforms just to promote themselves, the effectiveness of the platform will be reduced for everybody.

Yet this trend exists. The most interesting campaign is probably Ubuntu Edge. I've spoken briefly about them in the book, but they deserve their own true story.

True Story: Ubuntu Edge When $12 Million Is Not Enough

To run an efficient team, you only need three people: a Hipster, a Hacker, and a Hustler.
– REI INAMOTO, Chief Creative Officer for AKQA

Ubuntu Edge is not a campaign on Kickstarter but on Indiegogo. Yet they are one of the most interesting examples of failed crowdfunding . . . that could have succeeded. This campaign raised over $12 million and still failed because they set an unrealistic goal of $32 million.

First of all, "unrealistic" is not necessarily a bad word for a tech startup. PayPal, Amazon, and Google all set unrealistic goals and they all succeeded in changing the environment for many to follow. Today Elon Musk–founder of PayPal–plans the "unrealistic" goal of sending families to Mars in less than a generation, and I cheer his success.

Ubuntu Edge was about producing a handset as powerful as a laptop but the size of a smartphone, running with OS Ubuntu and Android. I loved this idea and I pledged to the project, however even an enthusiast like me was almost sure that the project was going to fail. $32 million is simply too much for niche technology.

In some cases the project owner sets an impossible goal to reach in order to enjoy the free promotion. They are not ready to create the product so they use a famous crowdfunding platform to "test the water" and create some buzz for the future. I don't know if this was the case of Ubuntu Edge, but when the campaign closed the page showed an incredible 139,000 Facebook shares and 13,300 Tweets. Plus all the articles published by bloggers and the discussions on social media.

Whatever the truth–extreme miscalculation or extreme manipulation–I hope they'll try again. Luck protects the bold . . . up to a certain point.

Campaigns from This Chapter

- Ubuntu Edge (by Canonical)
  http://igg.me/at/ubuntuedge

12. The Secret of Reddit

You can't learn in school what the world is going to do next year.
– HENRY FORD

Reddit.com is the popular sharing website created by Alexis Ohanian and Steve Huffman. The website is not a secret in itself but its use as a superb marketing tool seems to be unknown by many marketing consultants. I see thousands of dollars spent every day on Google Adwords and Facebook ads, but not much on low cost campaigns on Imgur and Reddit. Probably because both sites require creativity and money alone are not enough.

If you are not familiar with Reddit, the public shares links, posts and images divided into categories (the "subreddits"). There is a subreddit for every major subject (books, movies, science, etc.). Are you into games? Then you can share your passion with reddit.com/r/gaming. And so on.

Even better, there are many specific and unusual communities, such as "/aww" dedicated to pictures of "puppies, bunnies, and other things that make you go AWW" or "/hackedgadgets" for "gadget-surgeons, build enthusiasts".

A few days or weeks before the campaign starts, go to

Reddit Search (www.reddit.com/search) and find all the communities potentially interested in your product.

Think about Petcube, a webcam for cats (yes, you heard that right). They raised $251,000 equal to 251% of their goal. Their video could make a killing in any community related to pets and gadgets. Five seconds spent posting a link to the video can direct hundreds of potential customers to your Kickstarter page and generate a great deal of social media sharing.

P.S. – If you like this tactic, you should have a look to StumbleUpon.com as well.

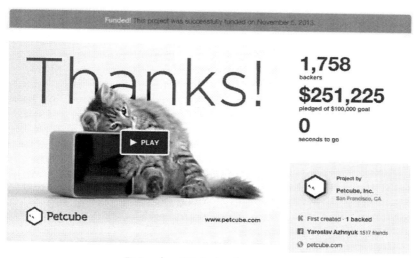

Petcube Kickstarter page

6 Things to Do After the Campaign Ends

What Happen When the Campaign Ends?

Once you have experienced the thrill of flight, when you're back down to earth, you will continue to look at the sky.
– LEONARDO DA VINCI

First of all "ends" is the wrong word. Even if the campaign has been unsuccessful there is still a chance of generating some good business from it. We'll talk about this later.

If your project has been funded, this is not the end but the start of your business. When the time runs out two major possibilities arise:

1. You can use your success story to generate more business,
2. You can transform your backers into long term repeat customers.

In the following pages you can find a list of actions that will help you capitalise on these opportunities.

1. Transform Kickstarter into Your Personal E-commerce

You've found market price when buyers complain but still pay.
– PAUL GRAHAM, Co-founder of Y Combinator

The page of a successful campaign always receives traffic. If you can convince any journalists or bloggers to write about your success story the traffic can be massive and it doesn't end with the campaign. The blog posts will be around for a while, in theory forever. Visitors can't back a closed campaign but you can still sell to them by putting a link to your website at the top of the description.

See an example from Pebble's page. The campaign has long since closed–years ago in fact–but the page is still bringing in valuable business for the company.

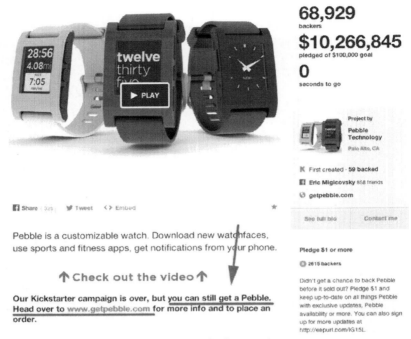

68,929
backers

$10,266,845
pledged of $100,000 goal

0
seconds to go

Project by
Pebble
Technology
Palo Alto, CA

First created · **59 backed**

Eric Migicovsky 858 friends

getpebble.com

See full bio   Contact me

Pebble is a customizable watch. Download new watchfaces,
use sports and fitness apps, get notifications from your phone.

↑ **Check out the video** ↑

**Our Kickstarter campaign is over, but you can still get a Pebble.
Head over to www.getpebble.com for more info and to place an
order.**

Pledge $1 or more

2615 backers

Didn't get a chance to back Pebble
before it sold out? Pledge $1 and
keep up-to-date on all things Pebble
with exclusive updates, Pebble
availability or more. You can also sign
up for more updates at
http://eepurl.com/IG15L.

Pebble's Kickstarter page links to their ecommerce

Unfortunately you can't edit your page after the
campaign has closed. If you do want to make post-
campaign changes it is best to do so a few minutes before
the deadline expires.

If you miss the deadline you can try contacting the
Kickstarter team and asking them to make the change on
your behalf. They're not obliged to do so, and it's not a
guarantee, however I've seen many successful cases.

2. Convert Your Backers into Long Term Customers

There are few overnight successes and many up-all-night successes.
– Anonymous

Surprise your backers with a handwritten note or other personal touch. They have invested in you after all, and you didn't even have a product at the time! Trust is already there, making it easier to convert them into long term repeat customers.

Moreover your backers can be your best promoters: they want to prove to their friends that they are good at picking winners! Surprise them with your attention to detail or an unexpected personal touch, and many of them will talk about you to their friends, generating free viral advertising.

This doesn't have to be expensive or sophisticated. Just find a gift that compliments your style. Doug and Jimmy of Minaal—the two New Zealanders from our case study—still send me funny emails every now and then.

The Satellite Gallery, a group of art students from Vancouver, a city I love, sent an extra picture with a handwritten thank you note. If you are not convinced that this tactic is worth your effort, just think about the lines you have just read. I am writing about Minaal and the Satellite Gallery because they were different, indirectly promoting both of them free of charge.

3. Managing Delays: Kill Two Birds with One Stone

You never know how strong you are until being strong is the only choice you have.
– BOB MARLEY

Almost every campaign on Kickstarter suffers some delays. Backers expect this but it doesn't mean that they are comfortable with it. If there is a delay use your Kickstarter page to keep customers and backers updated. Not only do they deserve it but you'll also be killing two birds with one stone.

First of all, by being kept up-to-date you reduce the risk of your backers sharing negative comments on your Twitter feed for all to see.

Secondly, the ping could motivate a few of them to talk about your project with their friends: an excellent opportunity to promote your post-Kickstarter business to new potential customers.

Beyond Delays

The emailing platform at Kickstarter should not be

limited to important updates or to notify of delays. If some time has passed without any contact, message your backers anyway. Send them a picture of your team working for them, or send them a funny story. They are not just customers; quoting Seth Godin "they are your tribe."

4. A Couple of Administrative Tips

Running a startup is a like being punched in the face repeatedly, but working for a large company is like being water boarded.
– PAUL GRAHAM, Co-founder of Y Combinator

After time has run out, and your campaign has been successful two things may happen and you might be in for a couple of nasty surprises.

1. Kickstarter charges the backers' credit cards. But the backer can still contest the payment with the credit card company. Or, they could have cancelled their backing just before the end of the campaign. Fingers crossed that this is not going to happen but do be prepared to receive around 10% less than you expected.

2. If you receive payments by PayPal there is a small risk of the funds being frozen "pending investigation". I am a big fan of PayPal, but they can be picky sometimes. I have seen at least two cases where the campaigners had their funds temporarily frozen.

If this happens contact PayPal's customer support in

a firm but polite way. Never ever be rude. You don't want to pick a fight with the biggest kid on the block! (On the other hand, if you've reached a stalemate, one or two complaining tweets might help. Just saying!)

5. Selling Through Kickstarter After Kickstarter

A good traveler has no fixed plan, and is not intent on arriving.
– LAO TZU, The Way of Life

For the same reason why many backers want to be kept informed in advance about campaigns coming soon—and register for a newsletter that tells them that—many want to be able to purchase the product after the campaign is finished. Whatever the reason, they have missed the campaign and they don't want to wait until the product is on the market for all customers or pay the (usually) higher official price. In fact they want to join that first batch of shipments reserved for the backers.

Some websites like BackersHub (http://bit.ly/ backersh) fulfils such demand. Dwight Peters, creator of BackersHub, matches closed campaigns and repeat backers.

If you have just concluded your campaign, you could consider expanding the number of backers through BackersHub or a similar website.

6. Or Sell Your Entire Company

Don't start a company unless it's an obsession and something you love. If you have an exit strategy, it's not an obsession.
– MARK CUBAN, Serial Entrepreneur and Investor

Before your partners become too excited let's face it; selling a company after a Kickstarter campaign is very uncommon, and sometimes despicable. Many founders start a company with the idea of selling out fast only to fail miserably.

Yet these acquisitions are less and less uncommon. There is a growing trend of exits post-Kickstarter where a small tech company has been acquired by a giant such as Facebook. The founders of these companies didn't want to sell out fast; in fact they built a remarkable product to last. That's the secret of their success. A remarkable product with a remarkable team is an attractive target for a big corporation.

Sometimes these operations are called "acquihires" (acquisition + hiring) because big companies like Yahoo or Google want to absorb the small company's team more so than their customers.

Two examples:

1. Oculus Rift acquired by Facebook
2. Matter acquired by Medium (founded by Evan Williams, founder of Twitter)

I'll say it again. It's highly unlikely that you are going to sell your company after Kickstarter, but it's a trend that you should be aware of. If Kickstarter can arouse interest from the founders of Facebook and Twitter your company could find investors and media exposure.

True Story: Oculus Rift

It doesn't matter how many times you fail. You only have to be right once and then everyone can tell you that you are an overnight success.

— MARK CUBAN, Serial Entrepreneur and Investor

I would be very surprised if you have never heard about Oculus Rift. Even if you don't remember the name you will have seen the product in the thousands of articles and interviews written about it.

Oculus Rift is a virtual reality headset. The main initial target was made for gamers, but a virtual reality helmet at an affordable cost has endless possibilities: architects, trainee doctors, even some branches of the military, and much more.

Oculus was purchased by Facebook approximately a year after their campaign for around $2 billion. Two thousand million. The sum is surprising but the acquisition was not completely unexpected by insiders.

I am not going to write a long chapter about Oculus Rift. You have probably read about them already. Have a look at their page, check their video, the updates and the two thousand plus comments. Every part of the campaign is a great example of how to manage a project on Kickstarter.

I just want to stress one point. Oculus didn't build a company to sell out fast. On the contrary, they worked with maniac-like obsession to create a remarkable product. And the entire team acted like a successful tech company from day one. From the outside they looked like a large team with everything under control, while I'm sure the reality was quite different.

In some campaigns playing the underdog or naive engineer works very well. But you can't play this card if you have a high technology product aimed at the mass market. In this situation you need to be seen as extremely reliable.

Campaigns from This Chapter

•   Oculus Rift: Step Into the Game (by Oculus)
    http://kck.st/NU6QRn

True Story: Matter and Medium

The best revenge for rejection is success.
– MARK SUSTER, Serial Entrepreneur and Venture Capitalist

Matter was an online magazine with a great twist. In a world where every news website focuses on publishing a large number of posts every day, usually from unpaid bloggers, the mission of Matter was to publish just one top-tier long-form article per week. Jim Giles and Bobbie Johnson, the founders, detailed their philosophy on the campaign page:

"Good journalism isn't cheap: it takes time and money for great reporters to do their best work. That means we're going to have to charge. But not much: we're aiming for around 99 cents per story. It's an experiment to see if independent journalism, done right, can fill the gap left by mainstream media."

As a backer I love the idea and clearly I was in good company. Matter reached their initial target in just two days, and closed at an exceptional 280% of the target.

As an entrepreneur, I take the opposite view. It can't work (but I hope I'm wrong). It ends up that I was right and wrong at the same time. Matter was not generating enough revenue to survive and expand, but Kickstarter has been an inestimable help in getting great media exposure

Long story short, they got noticed by Medium.com, a free publication platform founded by Evan Williams, formerly founder of Twitter. At the time Medium was growing, but the content was not enough.

Matter is not a billion dollar acquisition like Oculus Rift, Evan Williams says that "they joined forces". And yet, doing the job you love and working with the founder of Twitter is a great success in itself, at least for me. Don't you think?

Campaigns from This Chapter

- Matter (by Jim Giles, Bobbie Johnson and Matter) http://kck.st/Aonvvh
- Evan Williams, founder of Twitter, writes about how he stumbled across Matter on Kickstarter https://medium.com/about/big-stories-matter-aca87b5ec646

Kickstarter UK for Non British

How to Apply for Non British People

And then there is the most dangerous risk of all. The risk of spending your life not doing what you want on the bet you can buy yourself the freedom to do it later.
– RANDY KOMISAR, The Monk and the Riddle

Over the last few years, many young European entrepreneurs have been moving to the UK and fundraising on Kickstarter or through private investors. Doing business in the UK has become very popular, unfortunately being popular doesn't mean being simple.

Moving to the UK is easier than moving to other European countries, still you need to set up a company (very easy), open a bank account (not totally easy) and– because of Kickstarter's requirements–have a UK resident as a project representative (this could be hard if you don't have someone who trusts you completely – and vice versa).

Let's make a summary of those requirements:

UK REQUIREMENTS SCHEME

1. UK company: no limits

As a general rule, citizens from any country in the world can open a company in the UK, even those from outside Europe. In theory, it's possible that your country may have some probation, but not if you are part of the European Union. If you are a citizen of a Member State, you have no restriction to travel and do business in any other EU country. I'm not always a fan of the Union, but I will praise the founding fathers for that specific freedom.

2. UK company director: no limits

Unless your country has a ban against the UK, you should be able to be the company director. These bans are very rare–I've worked with over 50 countries and never had an issue–and they are practically impossible if you are a citizen of the European Union.

#TIP – When you open your bank account the bank will require a meeting with all the company directors. When you set up the company, you could consider appointing only one director. This is not mandatory, and most of the startups I follow have more than one director.

However, it could be more difficult and more expensive to find a day when the bank and 2-3 directors are in town.

3. Bank account: in theory no limits

But in practice it can be very hard to open a bank account if at least one director is not a UK resident.

Note: the director doesn't have to be a UK citizen; he just needs to live in the UK as a resident. If you don't have one you need to convince the bank that there is a genuine reason why a group of foreigners want to set up their company outside their country (and no "tax is lower here" is not an acceptable answer).

Personally, we have always succeeded. But I was there, talking to the bankers. I've seen many startups look shady just because their English wasn't good and they were incapable of a simple answer. This is a delicate subject, and I'll be writing a dedicated set of advice in the next chapter.

4. Campaign Referent: UK residents only

Every Kickstarter campaign should provide the name of one person as the campaign referent. It's not required that this person be a company director (although this could be a good idea for payment reasons) but in a way he/she'll be the director in the eyes of Kickstarter.

#**NOTE** – the director doesn't have to be a UK citizen; he just needs to live in the UK as a resident.

If you want to launch on Kickstarter UK you need one. Period! It could be a friend, an employee or a member of the team. Usually having a UK bank account and a UK utility bill in your name is enough. Kickstarter will not analyse the international pacts between your country and the UK. It's your duty to self certify the truth (and provide the bill above).

And no, before you ask, I can't be that person. Indeed I've been the director for some projects I like and some teams I know. But I'm not in the nominee business. I truly enjoy following a few campaigns and startups, from business model to marketing and more, and to keep my standards high I simply can't manage too many of them.

#**WARNING – Your representative can't be a backer**. Remind your representative NOT to buy any pledges on your campaign or you will lose everything. In fact, if your representative purchases a pledge, in a way he's paying himself. For credit card policies that was forbidden in the original US Kickstarter and it's been extended to Kickstarter in other countries.

How-to Apply for Non British Companies

A journey of a thousand miles begins with a single step.
– Chinese Proverb

If you are a non-British entrepreneur you probably already have a company in your country. Unfortunately this company will NOT be accepted by Kickstarter UK. To operate their crowdfunding you need a UK company.

We have spoken about setting up a UK company in the previous chapter; here we are going to describe the options in case you already have a non-British company. No matter where your company is based you have only three options:

1. You Can Start a Separate UK Company

You and your partners will be the only shareholders of the UK company. The existing foreign company will be kept out of the picture.

Most of the time the ownership in the UK company is a mirror of the non-British company (for instance, if you have 51% in the non-British company, you'll have 51% in the UK company). However, this is not mandatory. The shares could be different and that different split is a very good idea when you want to dedicate a person to Kickstarter. If you or one of your partners is in charge of the campaign, it's fair that he gets an extra percentage of the company as a bonus.

This separate UK company is usually the best solution when your Kickstarter product can be separated from your usual business. For instance if you develop apps for others and you want to launch a great game on Kickstarter, it's probably better to keep the two businesses separate. Your existing non-British company will keep working for B2B customers, while the UK company will focus on B2C games. In the future a separate UK company could look around for investors interested in gaming.

It's a clean start and if your campaign fails you can shut down the UK company with no damage to your existing company, or keep the UK company "dormant" for a minimum yearly cost to be used in the future.

2. Or You Can Start a UK Branch of Your Existing Company

The second alternative is to set up a UK company 100% controlled by your existing company. Or maybe your existing non-British company will have less than 100% to give a few bonus shares to your representative UK resident (for instance, 90% to your company and 10% to your UK friend). In both cases your UK company is a branch of your existing company.

From a corporate point of view that makes no sense because the UK is one of the best countries in Europe to manage shares and investors. The ideal scenario is the opposite, with the UK company open to investment and controlling your non-UK branch.

However, the reality could stop you for taking advantage of UK benefits. For instance, if your team leaves and work in Spain, and your customers are based in Spain as well it probably makes sense that your mother company is based in Spain and you just have a secondary branch in the UK dedicated to Kickstarter.

3. Or You Can Move Your Mother Company to the UK

You set up a UK company mirroring the shares of your existing non-British company then you have the UK company purchase all the shares of your existing company. The result: your UK company becomes your mother company, and your local company becomes a branch.

This solution could be particularly useful for tech

startups. In fact, having the mother company in the UK makes it easier to get investments (i.e. thanks to the SEIS scheme, your investors get 50%-70% back from their investment, up to £150,000).

We are speaking about corporate structure here, not tax. In fact, in the European Union anybody can set up a company anywhere, and yet taxes follow a different set of rules. For instance, you can open your company in the UK but if your team is in Belgium and your customers are in Belgium you will still pay taxes in Belgium. I've lived in Brussels and I agree that the local 50% tax could be scary for an entrepreneur. Still, that's how it works.

The usual disclaimer: This chapter is a corporate summary and it's based on a UK point of view. It's possible that your country would ask for extra requirements.

Before you decide which of the three solutions is best for you, have a serious consultation with a tax lawyer or an accountant in your country. This is not a law manual; you can tell that even by the price - fifty times cheaper than a legal book. You have been warned, right?

How-to Open a UK Bank Account for Non British Residents

No one remembers how you got there, only that you got there.
– JASON CALACANIS, serial entrepreneur and investor

Opening a company for a foreigner in the UK is extremely simple; unfortunately a bank account can be much more challenging.

In this age of global economy and global crimes banks have become very cautious. I've worked with over 50 jurisdictions and opening an account for a foreign small entrepreneur has always been at the very least not easy and often extremely painful.

From time to time a bank gets slapped by the regulators for not being zealous with their due diligence, or they have a change of management and they begin refusing non-resident customers. Don't worry too much, if your business is transparent, there will always be a bank looking for your money. The UK has a long tradition of international trading and they are relatively more open than many other countries.

The real issue is different. When it's a matter of opening a bank account, you can be your own worst enemy. I've seen many entrepreneurs explaining their business in such a confusing way to scare the poor bank manager. Not surprisingly, they had their application refused.

To reduce this risk, I've prepared a list of advice for our startups. Feel free to use it even if you are a traditional business, the list is valid for everybody. Don't be amazed if it sounds like common sense, sometimes it is.

#NOTE - In this case non-British means people non-resident in the UK. If you are a foreigner living in the UK, you should not have these problems.

1. Be Prepared to Fly

It's very unlikely that a bank will open your bank account without meeting you in person. By "very unlikely" I mean almost impossible. In fact according to money laundering regulations they are required to meet you and take a copy of your identity document.

First consequence: be prepared to make a trip to the UK. Schedule an appointment first.

Second consequence: be very careful about "consultants" promising to open a bank account without you being present. Even if this is true, they are probably in a different business. You are NOT in tax management; you have a "real" business.

Besides, if your campaign is successful, you or your partner may decide to move to the UK. This trip is a good opportunity to see if you like the place. If you run a tech startup go spend some time at the Google Campus or anywhere else you can find fellow founders. If you have a more traditional business size up the city (it does not have to necessarily be London).

If you don't like the place there are many other countries where you can try crowdfunding. A business is a great excuse for having a life experience in a different country. I admit I may be biased by my own life experiences. At least consider it.

2. Be Ready to Speak . . . English

If your English is bad bring someone with you. The bank manager is already a bit paranoid about opening an account for a non resident, don't make his life difficult or you are going to pay the consequences.

3. Get to the Point

Reply to their questions with clear answers. Get to the point. You can chat more if they ask. Here is a good answer:

"We have developed an innovative mouse (showing a sample). And we are moving to London because it is the best place in Europe to find investors."

4. He's a Bank Manager Not Your Counsellor

I wonder why so many entrepreneurs feel the need to annoy this poor manager with everything but their business, from intimate details of their life to their issues with English food (ok, I can understand the latter, it's just not the right time). Again, get to the point.

5. He's a Bank Manager Not a Venture Capitalist

At one point the manager is going to ask you a simple question.

"How much did you invest in the company?"

Fight the urge to impress him. This is especially common with programmers. A good developer can easily be paid £100 per hour; he has worked every night and weekend on his startup in the last 3 months, so 2 founders x £100/hour x 80 hours/week x 12 weeks =

£192,000. When the manager hears that almost £200,000 has been invested in the company he flicks a mental switch and immediately flags the company for a money laundering check. If you are lucky you will still get your bank account but it could take weeks.

The best answer is "We just invested our time, and a couple of hundred pounds of personal money".

I'm not saying that you have to lie but be realistic.

6. Don't "Sell" Investors That You Don't Have (Don't Sell Investors at All)

Another typical conversation I hear too often.

Founder: "We have found investors for $250,000, and they are ready to fund us as soon as the bank account is open".

Manager: "Great. According to the money laundering regulations, I need the names and passport numbers of these investors".

Ouch! You don't need to impress anyone. Opening a bank account is one of the most boring activities on earth. Don't try to make it exciting. Get to the point.

7. No Need to Bring Money

I've never seen a corporate account being opened on the same day. The bank needs to conduct due diligence and check on you and your business and–unfortunately– this could take days, sometimes more. So they will not request that you deposit cash into the account, because there is no account (yet).

We are speaking about foreigners with no existing corporate account in the UK.

One the contrary, if the UK resident working as your Kickstarter representative is also the sole director of the company, than you should not have the issues above. Everything is going to be easier (but you really need to trust him/her to give them sole access to the bank account).

8. Bring Every Director

The bank will want to meet all the directors. Even if only one administrates the account you should all be present.

9. Be Pessimistic (Just This Once)

When the bank asks for an estimate for your first

year's revenue there is no need to talk about raising millions from investors or hundreds of thousands of paying customers. Be restrained.

You may think that a bank manager is more prone to opening an account if you promise to deposit millions. The opposite is true. If millions flow into your account they will be required to work extra hard to control any risk of money laundering and–if you pass the regulations–they will lose you anyway. In fact the bank will move your company to a different department managing large corporate customers.

This is the only time as an entrepreneur where being pessimistic helps. Don't respond with the millions you dream of, but the worst case scenario.

10. One Day You'll Be a Big Corporation (but Not Now)

Opening foreign companies has been used (or abused) by many big corporations. The media regularly reports on some international company reducing their taxes through a sophisticated structure. Well, forget them.

You are not moving to another country for the same reasons. If your consultant talks more about taxes then building great products or growing your business it's probably time to change consultant.

If you are looking for crowdfunding then you are a small company, at best a medium-sized one. There is nothing wrong with that. Google was a small company for a while with the founders Larry Page and Sergey Brin working at a university. Apple headquarters was a garage for quite some time.

You'll grow eventually. In order to do that, you need a bank account. Play humble, it's just this one time.

#TIP – Take your passport to the bank, not your ID card. According to European regulation you can prove your identity with multiple documents: your passport, your national ID card and, sometimes, your driving licence. There's just one problem: banks can ignore that, and I understand their reasons. It's relatively easy to obtain a fake ID card or a fake driving licence, on the contrary passports are extremely difficult to forge. Therefore banks often refuse all documents but passports. The risk is simply too high. If you don't have a passport, consider to apply for one before your trip.

Resources for Setting Up a UK Company

It may be easier than ever to start a product, but building a company is just as hard as its ever been.
– SARAH LACY, Founder of Pandodaily

Resources

- **Companies House** – You can open a UK company by yourself through this website. Or you can appoint a company formation agent, a lawyer or an accountant.
  http://www.companieshouse.gov.uk/
- **HMRC** – This is the tax agency. You can use their website to request a VAT number and manage your accountancy, although it's probably better to leave this activity to an accountant.
  http://hmrc.gov.uk
- **Virtual Office** – Just pick the one you trust. Many of our companies start in London at The Hoxton Mix in Shoreditch, an area near Google

Campus and Tech City known for its many startups. Later they move to an accelerator or their own office.

http://bit.ly/virtualof

- **Invoicing and Accounting Software** – I've no doubts here. There is only one user-friendly software developed in the UK and tailored to UK companies: FreeAgent (10% discount voucher: 411f3958). Here is the short link: http://bit.ly/freeage

  An alternative. When I work with US companies, I use Xero. If you are already familiar with it, you may decide to use their UK version. In my opinion, Xero suffers in that it is made for another country and then adapted for the UK, but it's still a good alternative.

  There are many other online software, so the usual rule applies: use what YOU like the most. But be sure that it works properly in the UK. The majority of software is tailored for the US.

- **Accountant** – I have a conflict of interests here. I work with too many accountants and some of them are friends. Therefore I will not suggest a specific name.

  Use Google and word of mouth. You are a small company at this point, so don't aim for a famous firm but a transparent one. If they can't explain what services are included for what prices, then you should probably go somewhere else.

- **Shares and Investors Calculator** – If you want to have a look at possible company structure, or create the space for future investment, feel free to use our free calculator.

  http://startupagora.com/calculator

Templates

Media Database

This is the Google spreadsheet to be filled in by your virtual assistant. I can understand if you think that it's boring (I do) and yet you don't have a choice. Be prepared to spend hours per day on this list. Cheers!

You can download a spreadsheet version here:

http://startupagora.com/crowdfunding-template

P.S. – Pagerank and Alexa stats can be easily obtained through "Open SEO Stats" a free plugin for Chrome (or any other similar plugin). Just go to the Chrome web store:

http://chrome.google.com/webstore/category/apps

Columns

Step 1: Your virtual assistant fills this in.

- **Website** (i.e. John's Diary)
- **URL**
- **Name**
- **Surname**
- **Pagerank**
- **Alexa** (Global Rank)
- **Facebook** (followers)
- **Twitter** (followers)
- **Google Plus** (followers)

- **Newsletter** (followers. This information could be difficult to find. Tell the virtual assistant to leave it if she can't find the number on the website.)
- **Pinterest** (followers)
- **Relevant posts** (links to the relevant posts)
- **Notes**

Step 2: Then you fill this in

- **Mutual friends** (if any. P.S. – If you are brave enough you can give your Facebook password to the virtual assistant and ask her to check any connections. You can correct them later.)
- **Relevance** (how is this blogger relevant to your project? Rate them from 1 to 3 or from 1 to 5. Nothing more complex.)
- **Reach** (how easy is it to reach this blogger? For instance, do you have mutual friends? Are you a member of the same club?)

Blogger Sheet

Create a dedicated sheet for each major blogger: it will be extremely useful during the campaign. A major blogger doesn't necessarily mean a celebrity, but someone with a good number of followers connected to your area (i.e. they write about the same subject, or they wrote about similar projects, etc.)

Let the virtual assistant write the first version on a Google Doc and share with the entire team. You can eventually integrate the doc later.

To reduce the risks of data loss, usually most team members are authorised to view the document but forbidden to edit it.

Feel free to make any changes to the template but my suggestion is to not make it too complicated. This specific template has been proven in many campaigns.

Beware: the structure of the page may look strange in an eBook. In the original doc, the photo is on the left and the text is on the right.

– TEMPLATE –

Jodi Ettenberg | Legalnomads.com

[Censored]@gmail.com

Newsletter: YES

SOCIAL MEDIA (followers)

https://www.facebook.com/LegalNomads (25,300)

https://twitter.com/legalnomads (32,700)

https://plus.google.com/+JodiEttenberg (742,000)

http://instagram.com/legalnomads (11,800)

http://www.pinterest.com/jodiettenberg/ (2,500)

SHORT BIO

Food-obsessed world traveler, soup expert & former lawyer from Montreal.

MUTUAL FRIENDS

[censored]

RELATED POSTS

Interview: Minaal travel bag / Kickstarter

http://www.legalnomads.com/2013/10/thrillable-hours-doug-barber-minaal.html

NOTES

Eat gluten free, travel, love South East Asia.

— END —

First Contact

You never get a second chance to make a first impression.
– HARLAN HOGAN

"On my signal, unleash hell". I bet you recognise this quote from Russell Crow in the Gladiator. If you don't, take a break and watch the movie again. This is exactly how you should feel on day 1 of your campaign when you unleash your mass emailing to the list of contacts harvested over a month or so of hard work.

With a good organization and a bit of luck this first contact email could make your campaign. That's how we do it.

1. **First email to acquaintances and coworkers:** 1,000 plus identical emails sent on day 1 through Aweber (http://bit.ly/listaweber) or Mailchimp (http://bit.ly/listmailchimp). The conversion rate from this kind of email is limited, so you need quantity not just quality. If someone replies with interesting feedback, move him to Streak.com and and personalise your answer.

2. **First email to friends and family:** personalised emails prepared in the weeks before the beginning of the campaign and scheduled via

Streak.com to be sent together on day 1. The emails don't have to be completely different, but it's better (and respectful) if they are slightly different.

3. **First email to bloggers and journalists:** slightly personalised emails sent to the bloggers related to your business. These emails are prepared in the weeks before the campaign and scheduled via Steak.com to be sent together on day 1. It's very effective to add a link to at least one article written by the relevant blogger ("relevant" means that he writes about similar projects on Kickstarter or about the same market, etc). This is not flattery, you really need to read their articles and understand their style.

4. **First message to backers:** this is the only message not sent on day 1 but after you collect a few backers. They trusted you when you before anybody else, they deserve a warm thank you and they can become your best evangelist.

During the campaign you'll work non-stop to reply to questions and engage bloggers. Tools like Streak.com or Text Expander (http://bit.ly/textauto) can be helpful for preparing a template with the most common responses, enabling you to write them with one click. But most of the time the questions require a touch of personalization.

Day 1 of the campaign is different. You can prepare a mass emailing and many personalised emails weeks in advance and schedule them to be sent all together. Do it. It's boring and sometimes you'll feel a bit like a spammer, but it's one of the main pillars of your success.

First Email: Acquaintances and Coworkers

- **WHEN TO PREPARE THE LIST:** at least 2 weeks before the beginning of the campaign.
- **WHEN TO EMAIL:** On day 1 of the campaign. You can send a similar email around day 7 or when you have a new video or any other important update (insert the link to the video/update).
- **WHAT TOOLS TO USE:** This should be a massive emailing (we usually send over 1,000 emails). Use Aweber (http://bit.ly/listAweber) or Mailchimp (http://bit.ly/listMailchimp) or a similar service.
- **DO NOT** send this message from your email using the bcc field or it will be blocked for spamming (a disaster in the middle of a campaign).

The number 1,000 may look unattainable but it's not. Between you and your team you can reach the goal and celebrate this first achievement.

The conversion rate of this type of email is limited so you need quantity not just quality. You don't need current contacts, but anyone even remotely connected to your past. Check Gmail, Facebook and any other social media platform.

Feel free to adapt the text to your project and your

style, but don't make it too long. Get straight to the point. This is the first wave of emails and it should be short and simple. You have a chance to be more detailed and personalised when you answer the few people who write back.

#TIP - You can create a separated mailing list for every member of the team. This way every acquaintance receives a message from an email address he knows (but beware of duplicates. You don't want to send many copies to the same person). Making multiple lists is not mandatory, it's just an idea that you can ignore. However the conversion rate for multiple lists is usually 3-5 times higher than a single common list sent in the name of the company.

– TEMPLATE –

Subject: An important life update from [YourName]

Hi [Name],

I hope you are having an amazing day, because mine is looking quite weird.

I spent the last year developing a new [fantasy game / mouse with artificial intelligence / 3D printed earbuds / etc.] and today we are going public on Kickstarter. Don't laugh too much at our video:

http://kck.st/ProjectLink

I hope you can click the Facebook and Twitter buttons on that page to spread the word about our project. It may sounds cliché, but you can make a REAL difference for us.

This is not just business, I've invested one year of my life in this project together with an amazing team. Please send me any questions and feedback; I would really love to hear from you.

Cheers!

– [YourName]

P.S. Please forward this email to anyone who may also be interested. We truly need your support.

First Email: Friends and Family

- **WHEN TO PREPARE THE LIST**: this is a short list of friends and family but the emails are personalised. Writing the list will not take much effort, but writing the emails will. I would suggest starting 2-4 weeks before the beginning of the campaign.
- **WHEN TO EMAIL:** On day 1 of the campaign. You can send a similar email every 1-2 weeks (amend the text and apologise for being persistent) and when you have a new video or any other important update (insert the link to the video/update).
- **WHAT TOOLS TO USE:** Streak.com or a similar service. Write a few emails per day before the campaign and program the sending for day 1. You are supposed to write semi-personalised emails (friends and family talk each other and they'll find out if you send the same identical message. They expect the personal touch).
- **DO** send one message for each friend and family member. The only exception is families (i.e. You can send the same email to your uncle, auntie and their son).

– TEMPLATE –

I can't really tell you how to personalise an email to your friends. You can always start with the template for acquaintances, personalize it and maybe add a dedicated suggestion. Some examples I've used in the past:

- "I remember that you are a valued member of [xzy] association. We totally fit them. Do you think we can be added to their newsletter? That would be awesome."

- "Do you still hang out with [xyz]? I think he has a blog in this area. Would be great if you can introduce me (only if it's ok with you)"

First Email: Bloggers

This template is more of an example rather than a text to be used in a mass mailing. Relevant bloggers are limited in number and difficult to engage. They deserve the effort of a one-on-one email. It's going to be time consuming, but it will pay off in the long run.

P.S. - I admit the tone is flattering, but I mean it. When I find a journalist interested in the same area of our campaign, following them is a pleasure. On the contrary if you lie just to boost their ego there is a high chance they'll find out. They are journalists after all.

– TEMPLATE –

Hi [Name],

I got your name from our mutual contact, [Name Surname]. He was right; I enjoyed your article "[Title]" on [Techcrunch] and I've started following you.

I think you may be interested about a unique product in the same area.

We are launching [ProjectName] a [pocket 3D printed / sci-fi game for iPhone / etc.] on Kickstarter. Our page (bit.ly/ProjectName) has a video, photos and more information.

This could be of interest to you because:

1. [Describe 1-3 main elements. NOT THE TECHNICAL FEATURES but something interesting for a journalist. For instance "We are the first to ...", or "It's designed by the award winning designer ..."

Feel free to ask me any questions. We also have HD photos; just let me know if you'd like them.

I am available on Skype tomorrow (Thursday) at 2pm GMT and again at 6pm GMT. My Skype account is [SkypeName]. Or suggest a different time.

Thanks in advance for your time. It would be a great pleasure to hear back from you.

Cheers

– [YourName]

First Email: Backers

This message is sent to the initial backers when a milestone is reached. Feel free to personalise the style. Just remember that you don't have access to the backers' emails, but you can use the messaging tool in Kickstarter.

– TEMPLATE –

Hey there,

I just want to send a warm thank you for backing our project. You believed in us when we were unknown to many. After one week, we got coverage in Techcrunch, AOL and over one hundred tweets, not to mention over 500 backers and over $100,000. This result would not have been possible if you hadn't shown belief in our project at the beginning.

We owe you.

If you have any question or curiosity, feel free to drop me a message. Anytime ,anywhere. I mean it. Cheers!

– [YourName]

P.S. It would be great if you could share our campaign

link on Facebook: [http://kck.st/ProjectLink]

Autoresponder

This message is setup as an autoresponder to our emails from day 1 of the campaign.

– TEMPLATE –

Hey,

Thanks for contacting us. I'm proud to tell you that our Kickstarter campaign is online: [http://kck.st/ProjectLink].

Our [pocket 3D printed / sci-fi game for iPhone / etc.] is doing great however this can cause us to be a bit slower than usual to reply to emails.

If you would like to write about our project you can find all the information here: [http://YourWebsite/press].

Hope to chat/email with you soon.

Cheers

Virtual Assistant Email

I can't stress enough the importance of providing detailed instructions AND a deadline to your virtual assistant. Don't worry if the email looks like a manual for dummies, a smart VA will not be offended, in fact you are just making their job easier while reducing the risk of mistakes.

A virtual assistant doesn't share your office, and sometimes they work in a different time zone. They don't know your product yet, and they don't have your expertise. Managing an assistant like a co-founder is a recipe for disaster, so find an extra 10 minutes to write down every detail. It's quite boring at the beginning, eventually it will become far quicker and natural.

One Template to Rule Them All

There are too many variables to write a template for every possible email to your VA, however once you grasp the style you'll be fine. If you have a suggestion for other templates, contact me. I am always glad to share new ideas.

– TEMPLATE –

Subject: Compiling a list of bloggers

Hi Marianne,

I have a list of Kickstarter campaigns and I need to find bloggers who have written about them. Please note: when I use the word "blogger" I mean anyone publishing articles online (bloggers, journalists, etc.)

Here is what you need to do:

1. Go to http://kck.st/RXG0Z8

2. Save 3 images to your computer. Pick the images that you believe a blogger would have used in his post.

3. Go to Google Image Search http://www.google.com/imghp

4. Click the little camera icon (see Attachment-01.png) > Then click "Upload an Image" > Upload one of the image above (Alternatively you can drag the image directly into the search bar)

5. You'll be shown a list of web pages that used that image. (Ignore the field "Visually similar images" at the bottom of the page). Check each link on the first five pages. If they are blog posts copy the page URL to the

shared Google doc "Media List".

6. Copy the details of the blogger/journalist into the shared Google doc (I've completed the first two rows as an example for you).

7. To fill in the columns "Pagerank" and "Alexa" you can use "Open SEO Stats" a free plugin for Chrome. Just go to the Chrome web store: http://chrome.google.com/webstore/category/apps

8. To fill in the column about the social media followers go to each of their social media profiles.

9. Repeat points 4 to 8 for each image

As soon as you've finished, send me an email, and I'll send you more campaigns to check.

You should complete the task in 24 hours maximum. If you have any problems, please let me know immediately by email. Don't wait, just send me a message.

Thanks in advance

Stefano

Attachment-01

Useful Links and Resources

True Stories and Case Studies

(In alphabetical order)

1. Amanda Palmer: The new RECORD, ART BOOK, and TOUR (By Amanda Palmer)
   http://kck.st/JliwH9
2. Bring Reading Rainbow Back for Every Child, Everywhere! (By LeVar Burton)
   http://kck.st/1kKwSrD
3. Double Fine Adventure (by Double Fine and 2 Player Productions)
   http://kck.st/A9k3jH
4. Ego Smart Mouse (by Laura Sapiens)
   http://kck.st/13jNyOV
5. Elevation Dock: The Best Dock For iPhone (By Casey Hopkins)
   http://kck.st/uu4Ty8
6. Good & Proper Tea: London-based loose-leaf brew bar (By Emilie Holmes)
   http://kck.st/WZWZQl
7. Loka: the world of fantasy chess (by Alessio Cavatore and Mantic Games)
   http://kck.st/X2Paci
8. Matter (by Jim Giles, Bobbie Johnson and Matter)
   http://kck.st/Aonvvh

9. Metal Gear Solid: Philanthropy
   New movie: coming soon
   Existing movie (2009):
   http://bit.ly/mgs-p
10. Minaal Carry-on: travel faster, happier & more productive (By Doug Barber and Jimmy Hayes)
    http://kck.st/14YVmaZ
11. Oculus Rift: Step Into the Game (by Oculus)
    http://kck.st/NU6QRn
12. OwnPhones: Wireless, Custom-Fit, 3D Printed Earbuds (by Itamar Joban and others)
    http://kck.st/1p6JuZQ
13. Pebble: E-Paper Watch for iPhone and Android (by Eric Migicovsky and Pebble Technology)
    http://kck.st/HumIV5
14. Petcube - Stay closer to your pet (by Yaroslav Azhnyuk and Petcube Inc)
    http://kck.st/1b2kop5
15. Prodigy the Game (by Hanakai Studio and Jean Bey)
    http://kck.st/1lnbPdu
16. RAIN: a fan film about Storm (by Maya Glick)
    http://kck.st/1sLbw3a
17. Reaper Miniatures Bones II (by Reaper Miniatures)
    http://kck.st/1712ejw
18. Rebuild: Gangs of Deadsville (by Sarah Northway)
    http://kck.st/1bomFhU

19. SCiO: Your Sixth Sense. A Pocket Molecular Sensor For All (by Consumer Physics, Inc.)
http://kck.st/1hPqZ6I

20. SHADOW | Community of Dreamers (By Hunter Lee Soik)
http://kck.st/16asGpx

21. Soma - Beautifully innovative all-natural water filters (by Soma)
http://kck.st/VjAFva

22. Star Citizen (by Chris Roberts)
They raised $55 million on a proprietary platform:
http://robertsspaceindustries.com
An initial round of "just" $2.1 million was raised on Kickstarter:
http://kck.st/RXGoZ8

23. Start Trek: Axanar (by Axanar Production and Alex Peters)
http://kck.st/1xcoBwr

24. Stem Cell Trial for Multiple Sclerosis (by Tisch MS Center)
http://igg.me/p/696737/x/2082976

25. The Coolest Cooler (by Ruan Greeper)
First campaign (unsuccesful):
http://kck.st/1hfaWUu
Second campaign:
http://kck.st/1oweGkH

26. The Great Kingdom, the Creation of Dungeons & Dragons (by Andrew Pascal and Others)

https://www.kickstarter.com/projects/
720223857/the-great-kingdom

27. The Seed (by Misery Dev. Ltd and Nicolai Aaroe)
http://kck.st/1mfsx19

28. The Veronica Mars Movie Project (by Rob Thomas)
http://kck.st/Z1HJRR

29. Ubuntu Edge (by Canonical)
http://igg.me/at/ubuntuedge

30. Urban Heroes (by Tin Hat Games)
http://kck.st/PweJ4N

Resources and Tools

#NOTE – I am not into the business of affiliate marketing. All the links below are companies that we use or good competitors. A few of them pay a small amount of money as an affiliate commission. I don't keep these commissions, they are used to support young startups.

(In alphabetical order)

1. **Aweber** – One of the most popular mass emailing services among bloggers
   http://bit.ly/aweberUrl

2. **BackersHub** – Sell your product to backers after Kickstarter
   http://bit.ly/backersh

3. **Boomerang** – Schedule an email to be sent later (Free for Gmail, requires a subscription for Google Apps)
   http://www.boomeranggmail.com/

4. **Cybranding.com** – Find influencers and hashtags for your campaign
   http://bit.ly/Cybranding

5. **FreeAgent** – UK accounting and invoicing
   10% discount code: 411f3958
   http://bit.ly/freeage

6. **Hashtagify.me** – Free hashtag analysis (Free tool)
   http://bit.ly/Hashtagify

7. **Hootsuite** – Schedule, manage, measure your social media
http://bit.ly/socialmana

8. **Mailchimp** – One of the most popular mass emailing services among big companies
http://bit.ly/mailchimpUrl

9. **Mailtrack.io** – Know when your email are read (Free tool)
http://mailtrack.io

10. **Optimizely** – A/B testing made it simple.
http://bit.ly/optimizel

11. **PickFu** – Real consumer feedback in minutes
http://bit.ly/pickf

12. **Prefundia** – Crowdfunding "coming soon" platform
http://bit.ly/prefundia

13. **Shares and Investors Calculator**
http://startupagora.com/calculator

14. **Streak** – CRM software working inside Gmail. Schedule an email to be sent later, create templates and more.
(Free tool)
https://www.streak.com

15. **Talkwalker Alerts** – Easy alternative to Google Alerts
(Free tool):
http://www.talkwalker.com/en/alerts

16. **Text Expander** – Write long text with one click

http://bit.ly/textauto

17. **Voice Bunny** – Get fast, professional voice overs you'll love
http://bit.ly/voicebun

Specific Resources for UK Companies

- **Companies House** – You can open your company here, trough a company formation agent or trough a lawyer or accountant.
http://www.companieshouse.gov.uk/

- **HMRC (Tax Agency)** – You can request a VAT number here, and manage your accountancy. However, you probably want to leave this to your accountant.
http://hmrc.gov.uk

- **Virtual Office** – You probably want to start with a low cost virtual office, before you move to the UK. Most of our startups use an office in Shoreditch–the startup area–near Google Campus and Tech City. However, there are many good provider in London (and many bad unfortunately). Just pick the one you trust the most. This is the virtual office we usually use:
http://bit.ly/virtualof

- **Invoicing and Accounting Software** – I've no doubts here. There is only one user-friendly software developed in the UK and tailored to UK companies: FreeAgent (10% discount voucher: 411f3958). Here is the short link:

http://bit.ly/freeage

An alternative. When I work with US companies, I use Xero. If you are already familiar with it, you may decide to use their UK version. In my opinion, Xero suffers in that it is made for another country and then adapted for the UK, but it's still a good alternative.

There are many other online software, so the usual rule applies: use what YOU like the most. But be sure that it works properly in the UK. The majority of software is tailored for the US.

- **Accountant** – I work with too many accountants and a few of them are friends. I'm in a conflict of interests here, therefore I will not suggest a specific name. Use Google and word of mouth, when you do your diligence remember a basic rule valid for every professional: ask for transparency. If they can't explain what services are included for what prices, then you should probably not appoint them.

- **Shares and Investors Calculator** – If you want to have a look to possible company structure, or live the space for future investment, feel free to use our calculator. We have prepared it for our own startup, so no charge apply. It's free. http://startupagora.com/calculator

Contact

My update contact details are on my website. http://startupagora.com/help

Printed in Great Britain
by Amazon.co.uk, Ltd.,
Marston Gate.